BOUNDARY POWER

By Mike O'Neil:

Power to Choose: Twelve Steps to Wholeness

By Mike O'Neil and Charles E. Newbold:

The Church as a Healing Community: Setting up Shop to Deal with the Pain of Life-Controlling Problems

For information on ordering books, videos or tapes, write:

Power Life Resources
2601 Pulley Road
Nashville, Tn. 37214

or call (615) 872-0098

Contents

BOUNDARY POWER

How I Treat You
How I Let You Treat Me
How I Treat Myself

Mike S. O'Neil
CAODAC, NCAC I

Charles E. Newbold, Jr.
M. Div.

A POWER LIFE RESOURCE
from
Sonlight Publishing, Inc.

The authors gratefully acknowledge permission to use material from the following:

Boundaries: Where You End and I Begin by Anne Katherine, published by Parkside Publishing, Park Ridge IL. C 1991 Hazelden Foundation, Center City, Minnesota.

Taken from the book Boundaries: When to Say YES, When to Say NO, To Take Control of Your Life by Dr. Henry Cloud and Dr. John Townsend. Copyright C 1992 by Henry Cloud and John Townsend. Used by permission of Zondervan Publishing House.

From Emotional Incest Syndrome by Dr. Patricia Love. Copyright C 1990 by Patricia Love and Jo Robinson. Used by permission of Bantam Books, a division of Bantam Doubleday Dell Publishing Group, Inc.

Sexaholics Anonymous published by SA Literature, P.O. Box 111910, Nashville, TN, 37222. Copyright C 1989 SA Literature. Reprinted with permission of SA Literature. Permission to reprint does not imply SA affiliation or SA's review or endorsement of this publication.

Faces of Rage by David Damico, published by NavPress, Colorado Springs,CO. C 1992 by David Damico.

Anecdotal illustrations are fictional, though based on real situations, or are used with permission of the person involved.

All scripture quotations are taken from the King James Version of the Bible, with certain words changed to their modern equivalent; for example, "thou" has been changed to "you," and "saith" has been changed to "says."

published by

Sonlight Publishing, Inc.
2601 Pulley Road
Nashville, Tn. 37214
(615) 872-0098

ISBN 0-9633454-2-7
Seventh Printing
Printed in the United Sates of America

Acknowledgments

Major portions of this book were taken from Mike's lectures on boundaries. The personal stories in first person are his unless otherwise indicated. In addition to his own experiences and insights, two important resources for these lectures were *Boundaries: When to say YES, When to Say NO, To Take Control of Your Life*, by Dr. Henry Cloud and Dr. John Townsend, and *Boundaries: Where You End and I Begin*, by Anne Katherine. Charles included other significant resources as well as his own perceptions and experiences.

We express our great appreciation to those laborers who have gone before and plowed this important field of personal growth and recovery.

Both authors also write from their personal perspectives—how these principles have enhanced recovery in their own lives, effectively helped them to work their own boundary issues, and improved relationships. It is our hope that this book will do at least as much for you.

I will listen

I'm hear to listen
to what you have to
say — but I'm not
available for abuse
but I will come back
in ___ min, + talk to you.

consistency — do it over +
over again
I'm not available for abuse

I've worked very hard to improve
my relationship with you.

set my boundaries w/ Audrey + hexie

–1–

Introduction:
Intimacy in Relationships

*T*wo well-dressed men talk while having a cup of coffee. One turns to the other and says, "Man, I didn't know that there was so much wrong with me until I got married."

A wife says to the marriage counselor, "He's not the man I married." The husband breaks in and answers, "Honey, I never was."

A seductive man confides in his female co-worker, "My wife doesn't understand me. She doesn't know my needs."

A wife bashes her husband at the ladies luncheon, "He never pays any attention to me. He's all wrapped up in Monday night football."

A disappointed daughter cries when her dad backs out of seeing her act in the senior play, "But, Dad you promised."

A secretary says to her male boss, "I don't like it when you touch me that way."

These comments all have something to say about boundaries and boundary violations. They reflect problems in relationships. We need healthy relationships. Healthy relationships have much to do with intimacy. But we don't know how to have intimacy in relationships.

Intimacy is knowing and being known for who we really are in all aspects of our lives. It is being able to bring the truth of who I am to you, being received and accepted for who I am without your needing to fix me, and you being received and accepted by me for who you are without my trying to fix you.

But we have a problem! I have to know who I am before I can share me with you. You have to know who you are before you can share you with me. Neither of us know who we are because we were shamed out of our true sense of self as children growing up in our non-nurturing, dysfunctional families. We have, instead, created false selves who have emerged in these family situations in order to survive.

We survived until we could find a way of escape. Ironically, the way of escape turned out to be a revolving door. We walked back into the same kind of relationship we were trying to get out of. We took our little bruised, false selves out and met other little bruised, false selves and got into those relationships. We built our relationship on everything but intimacy. We built it on lust. We built it on the fact that we both like to go to the football games and party afterwards. We built it on being two very needy people.

We built it on my need to control you because you were a weak person. I didn't know I needed to control you or that you were a weak person, but my radar automatically sent me out to find you to get into a relationship with you. I thought I wanted a strong person but you ended up being weak, so I tried to get you to be what you were not. When you failed to change, it felt like you were no longer meeting my needs. So, we split up.

We mess up every relationship we get into. People abandon us or we end up abandoning them. The people who should be in our lives leave us, while the people who shouldn't be in our lives won't go away.

We want someone who understands how we feel, but we don't know how we feel. We want to feel close, but sex is as close as we can get. We want honesty, but false selves don't know honesty. We want trust but don't trust ourselves, so we project that distrust on to everyone else we know. We want to share our lives, but we don't know who we are in order to share them. We don't know how to give or how to receive in relationships.

These problems in relationships are due to the fact that we do not have healthy boundaries because we do not know who we are. We do not know who we are because our emotions were not properly mirrored for us during our formative years. Our families told us that what we saw was not what we saw, what we heard was not what we heard, what we felt was not what we felt—crazy-making stuff.

Now we come into adulthood. It's too late for our parents to do what they should have done for us at the only time those things could be done. If all the king's horses and all the king's men couldn't put Humpty Dumpty back together again, how can we, the broken pieces, ever expect to put ourselves back together again?

The task before us is not easy. We have to learn how to have healthy boundaries in relationships. To do that we have to know who we really are. We have to begin the arduous task of erasing all of the erroneous tapes that have been dictating our destructive behaviors in the past. Then, we can begin to reprogram ourselves with the truth of who we really are and can be.

Much of this process will begin to take shape as you move through this workbook. You'll learn about boundaries in the five major areas of your life—relational, spiritual, physical, sexual, and emotional. You will learn how to identify your boundary issues and those of others in your life, especially those who have been violating you. You should be able to envision yourself with healthy, firm boundaries that will set you free to be who you really are so you can take that and enter into real and intimate relationships with others.

Most of our problems and hurts in life involve relationships. Therefore, the solutions to these problems involve getting relationships right. The goal of this book is to attain boundary power in order that we might change how we treat others, how we allow others to treat us, and how we treat ourselves.

HOW TO USE THIS WORKBOOK

This workbook is not a scientific instrument for clinical diagnosis or treatment. It is, rather, a tool for self-evaluation and personal growth. Nevertheless, if you are in therapy, it can be a great tool for you.

We hope that you will be able to develop a reasonable "feel" for the kinds of boundary issues you may have. Moreover, we hope that this tool will provide some guidance to help you resolve the losses that past violations have caused. We also hope you will be able to redefine and strengthen healthy boundaries to avoid further loss in your life.

You can use this workbook individually, under therapeutic guidance, or with others in a group situation. We strongly recommend the group dynamic because it will enhance your growth experience. Group members can help clarify boundary issues, provide accountability, and give much needed support as you begin to set healthier boundaries in your relationships. If you are in a group, you are responsible for reading the text and doing the written work before each group session. Each chapter has a suggested group exercise with the exception of chapter 2, chapter 7, and chapter 17.

You will be asked numerous questions throughout this workbook which will help you inventory the state of your boundaries. These questions are expected to lead you into a deeper understanding of yourself as you progress toward the goal of resolving the losses that are associated with boundary violations. Answer the questions that apply to you personally. You will be challenged to think deeply about yourself at times. Take the time you need to be honest and thorough about yourself. Yet, do not get bogged down in any one question or section. If you don't know how to respond to a section, move on. You may discover the answers as you proceed. You may find yourself going back to answer questions you missed or change answers you've written previously.

This workbook is private. You alone are in charge of what you share about yourself from it.

GROUP EXPERIENCE

Group Leader:

1. Familiarize yourself with this book and the processes involved before going into your first meeting. Introduce yourself and set the agenda for these group meetings.

2. If the group members are new to one another, engage in a brief get-acquainted activity to help them feel comfortable and relaxed with one another.

3. Ask if there are any questions about the information in this chapter. Allow others to answer through group discussion.

4. Divide into small groups of three to five persons and have members state their names (first name only may be appropriate) and tell why they are here and what need they have to work on boundaries.

5. Bring the group back together. Ask for six to eight volunteers to form a tight circle. Put one volunteer in the middle and challenge him or her to break out of the circle. The volunteers forming the circle will close the gap as tightly as possible to keep that person from breaking out. Allow several to take turns in the circle.

Ask those within the circle: How did you feel trying to break out and failing? How did you feel breaking out?

Ask people in the circle: How did you feel trying to keep that person in?

Ask on-lookers: How did you feel about what you saw?

Reverse the process and ask volunteers to try to break into the circle. Follow the same procedure and ask similar questions.

Make note: The abuses that happen to us are all about relationships that either keep us bound in or shut out. Ask what insights others have after experiencing these exercises.

6. Ask for final questions, thoughts, and feelings that may need to be discussed before leaving.

Set time limits on these group sessions. Tell group members that they do not have to share anything they are not ready to share.

– 2 –

What Are Boundaries?

$\mathcal{M}$y father was a classic alcoholic, an absentee drunk. When he drank he usually left home. Drinking two quarts of vodka a day was mild. After three days you never knew he was drinking. If you couldn't smell him, you couldn't tell him. He was in and out of blackouts.

My mother was a classic codependent who had to be both mom and dad. I grew up in a home that had no boundaries. Figuratively speaking, we didn't have a door on the front or the back of our house. We called mother "Saint Erma, the martyr of Norman, Oklahoma" because she cared for everyone and anything—stray dogs, cats, stray humans, whatever. They came in the front door of our house and our lives, took what they wanted, then walked on out the back door. If they found somebody else that needed help, they'd bring them back with them the next time they came. My father was one of those people coming in and going out.

It was a classic alcoholic family. Though my father and mother both died sober, neither one of them knew anything about boundaries. Setting personal boundaries was a whole new concept for me as it is for many of us.

When it comes to relationships, Anne Katherine in her book, *Boundaries*, says that "a boundary is a limit or edge that defines us as separate from others." Boundaries define "where you end and I begin."[1] Drs. Henry Cloud and John Townsend in their book, also called *Boundaries*, turn it around and say, "where I end and someone else begins."[2] In either case, we can sum up boundaries in this one phrase: "I am not you." That is a powerful statement. When we are finally able to grasp that truth for ourselves, we will be well on our way to recovery from the damage that was done to us as result of the abuses in our lives.

My boundaries tell me who I am. Without a clear sense of boundaries, I am not going to know who I am. Boundaries and a sense of self go hand in hand. They are like maps that help us find our way down the road of life. They show us where the unsafe places are in relationships so we can avoid them, and they show us how to protect ourselves in all other areas of our lives.

A boundary violation, therefore, occurs "when one trespasses on the other's personhood, when one crosses a line and tries to control the feelings, attitudes, behaviors, choices, and values of the other" write Cloud and Townsend.[3] These violations can cross relational, physical, spiritual, sexual or emotional limits of another. It is difficult to make clear distinctions between these areas because an abuse in one area usually affects the other areas, too. A boundary violation is against the whole person: spirit, mind, emotion, will, and body.

Whether we know about boundaries or not, we still have some natural instincts for them. Otherwise, we would not be traumatized when our boundaries are violated. Something within us tells us that a certain action or attitude is wrong.

This idea of boundaries initially sounds like a fairly simple thing to understand, but as we move through this workbook, we will see how increasingly more entangled the issues become, especially when we begin to apply them in our lives.

— 3 —

Why Boundaries?

*M*ost of our problems in life have to do with relationships, and the source of these problems in relationships are most likely tied to boundary issues. We will continue to have problems in relationships if we do not establish healthy boundaries for ourselves. Learning about boundaries and learning how to practice healthy boundaries takes time. We will always have to pay attention to them in order to maintain them; otherwise, we may revert back into old boundary habits. They are not established automatically.

Boundaries tell us what is our business and what is not our business. It is our business what we think of ourselves and what we think of other people, but it is none of our business what others think of us (unless we have violated their boundaries and owe them amends). Many of us allow our lives to be manipulated by the fear of what others think of us.

This fear of what others think of us is an indication that we have created false selves. These false selves are the people we were led to believe others would accept and nurture. If anyone appears not to like us or accept us, we feel threatened because we fear rejection. We fear rejection because we've been rejected. We were rejected and our feelings were shamed during our developmental years. We were shaped by those no-talk rules in our non-nurturing, dysfunctional family: "It's not OK to say that."

Dad's drunk and the child says, "Dad's drunk!"

"No, Dad's not drunk, Dad's sick."

"Well, he fell down and passed out on the bathroom floor!"

"He likes to take a nap about this time of the evening, and that's just the way it is. He's not drunk and your father's not an alcoholic."

In other words, we didn't see what we saw, we didn't hear what we heard, and what we thought was going on, was not what was going on. Those are crazy-making messages for a child and contribute to the creation of a false self.

The child says, "I'm tired of Dad not being here because he works all the time. It makes me angry."

"Shame on you for feeling that."

"Well, OK, Mom, what feeling would you like me to have?"

"You should feel grateful."

"Oh, OK, I'll be grateful that Dad's never here because he works all the time and drinks the rest of the time."

The child is made to believe that Dad is working so much and working so hard because of the family's needs—that's what makes him drink too much.

"OK, now I'm supposed to feel grateful that he works, and guilty because it makes him drink, and ashamed because I feel angry, and rejected because what I think is going on is not what's really going on."

The little four or five-year-old is learning how to create a false self. When he's grown, his feet hit the floor every morning and it's, "HEYYYYY, Mister False Self is here. How are you?"

"Just fine, no problems at all."

"How 'bout some feelings?"

"No, thank you. All that stuff is too confusing for me."

We become who we think we are supposed to be and shame the person we really are. We live out our lives behind those masks. Then, we go find another false self to have a relationship with. We are incapable of having an intimate relationship with another person who is real. We are threatened by the prospects of intimacy. Our relationship is like two pieces of a puzzle. We find a perfect fit and it feels close because we fit so well. We're in LOVE. But there is no real intimacy. We're really "in sick" or "in heat." Together we seem to make one whole unit. But two half-people won't make a whole person. After a while the heat dies down between these two false selves, and she turns to him and says, "Well how do you feel?"

And he says, "Well, I think..."

"No, I didn't ask what you thought, I asked how you felt."

"It doesn't matter how I feel."

"Well, I don't think you love me."

"Of course I love you, I'm here, aren't I? I haven't left yet, have I?"

Eventually this couple may end up in counseling on their way to the divorce court. The counselor may ask, "Tell me about yourself, Mr. Jones. Who are you?"

"I work down at the mill over there, and I build these little widgets, and that's what I've done for the last twenty years, and I'll be retiring next year, and that's what I do."

"No, no, Mr. Jones. I asked you who you *are*. You told me what you *do*."

"What do you mean, 'Who am I?'"

"What do you like?"

"What's to like? You work, you pay bills, you sleep, you eat, you go back to work again."

"What do you do for fun?"

"I'm fifty-five years old. Fun is for kids. We don't do fun."

"What was the last thing you and your wife did for fun?"

"It was probably the year before we got married when we went to..."

Neither one of them can tell what they feel, think, want, or who they are. Their identities have been defined by this enmeshed, sick relationship they've been in for twenty years. All he knows is that he is sick and tired of her trying to fix him since the day they got married.

"I thought I was gonna, you know, get married and have a wife, and she'd

8

have a husband. I didn't know I was gonna be a project. And I can't seem to get it right no matter what, so I don't even try anymore."

The more he retreats, the more frustrated she gets and the harder she tries to bring them closer by trying to be who and what he wants. Eventually, she gets so frustrated that she gives up and retreats also. Sometimes she'll retreat to an affair, but eventually to a place of indifference toward him in order to avoid the pain associated with the relationship.

These situations involve boundaries. If we don't know what we feel, we can't know who we are. If we don't know who we are, we cannot tell someone else who we are. We will be false selves.

Here, then, are some of the reasons we need healthy boundaries.

Healthy boundaries define who we are.

Healthy boundaries can help us to know who we are. They can help us to have a better sense of our separateness from others: where we end and others begin.

Knowing who we are helps us to maintain a sense of reality. We will know who we are and are not, what we believe and don't believe, what we think, feel, like, and want.

Linda came in for counseling one day exasperated over her new-found revelation, "I just realized that I don't know what I like to eat. I have been buying food and cooking all of these years out of habit, and I've suddenly realized I don't even like the things I've been cooking and eating. I buy things in large volume just to save money, and I eat things I don't like, thinking it is the frugal thing to do. I know I don't like what I've been eating, but I don't know what I do like."

Knowing who we are, what we believe, what we think, feel, like, and want means that people can no longer walk in and out of our lives at will—using and abusing us.

Complete the sentences below describing, as much as you can, some of the most basic things you know about yourself—thoughts, beliefs, opinions, likes, dislikes, wants, etc. Add to this list as you think of things in the future. Make up your own sentences.

I am a (in relationship to others; for example, mother, father, brother, sister, etc.)

I am a (things you do; for example, coach, painter, photographer, hunter, swimmer, teacher, student, writer, dreamer, etc.)

I am (attributes and faults; for example, kind, helpful, selfish, stingy, pretty, ugly, stubborn, a push-over, etc.)

My best friend is

The things I like are

The things I like to do are

My favorite food is

My favorite restaurant is

My favorite color is

My favorite clothes are

My favorite TV choices are

The things (or people) I hate are

I believe God

Healthy boundaries define who we are in relationship to others.

Healthy boundaries are intended to help us have good relationships. Some relationships are of our choosing and some are not. Oftentimes we are stuck with relationships that are not of our choosing whether we like it or not. Some teenagers feel they are stuck with their parents. You may be stuck with people you don't like on the job, in the neighborhood, or in your religious group. Boundaries that define who we are help us to maintain our sanity in these unpleasant relationships. They help us to know what the extents and limits are with those with whom we are connected—how to let in what is good and keep out what is bad.

Other relationships, however, are of our choosing. Though we are stuck with our families of origin, as adults we have some say in who our family of choice will be. Healthy boundaries help us choose the relationships that we want to be in as well as those we don't want to be in. We don't have to be friends with everybody who shows up and says they want to be friends. We don't have to like everyone that we meet; everyone doesn't have to like us.

Name a few of the people with whom you are in a relationship but who were not of your choosing (family members, co-workers, neighbors, etc.).

Why would you not have chosen them?

Name a few of the people with whom you are in a relationship by your choice.

Who is someone you would like to have in your life but don't?

Why is he/she not in your life?

Healthy boundaries help us to know what thoughts, feelings, and behaviors are appropriate to have toward others in relationships.
We would not need boundaries if we were not in relationships. We have to be taught appropriate ways of thinking, feeling, and acting around other people.

We were supposed to have been taught those things by our caregivers during our developmental years, but many of us were not. So, we as adults have to learn for ourselves what is and what is not appropriate when it comes to our personal boundaries.

Tell about a time in your life when someone said or did something that left you feeling confused about what to think, feel, or do.

How did you resolve the confusion?

How do you typically resolve confusion?

Healthy boundaries help us to remove walls of defenses.

Things happen to us that are beyond our control. People do things that are wrong and offensive. We respond one of two ways to people when they do things to us. We will either re-act or pro-act. A re-action is a thoughtless, emotional response to the offense. A pro-action is a determined action resulting from a firm sense of boundaries. If we don't have boundaries, we are more likely to re-act than to pro-act. Our reactions will produce negative responses while pro-actions are more likely to produce positive responses.

If we don't have boundaries, our re-actions are either like walls or cannon balls. We'll either shut people out or blast them away.

Walls may seem like boundaries but they are not. They are defenses. We put up these defenses to distance ourselves in relationships. For example, we may hide behind joking, anger, silence, constant talking, or pretended ignorance. We relate to others over our walls. As we become experienced, we will begin to recognize our own and other people's defense mechanisms and develop healthy boundaries that break through these walls of defenses.

Name someone recently who has made you angry:

What did he or she do to make you angry?

What did you do with your anger?

Did you act on healthy boundaries or did you react with your defenses?

If you reacted, what defenses did you use?

How did the other person respond to your defenses?

Healthy boundaries free us to be who we are.

Healthy boundaries come from knowing who we are, and this frees us to be who we are. When we are free to be who we really are, we are better equipped to make our own choices instead of others making them for us. We can set our own boundaries. We are free from the control and manipulation of other people and free to do what we want to do for ourselves and for others.

Is someone other than yourself making the choices in your life that you think should be your choices?

What are some of those choices?

What would your choices have been?

Why are they making those choices instead of you?

Healthy boundaries enable us to be more accepting of others who are different from us.

The whole idea of boundaries in relationships is to define our separateness from others. Boundaries in relationships help us to be the unique individuals that we are. I am me. You are you. You can be who you are and I'll be who I am. You can be where you are in life and allow me to be where I am. If I know who I am and am confident in who I am, then I can allow you to be different from me and not be threatened by your differences.

We bring injury to one another when we fail to recognize that we have differences. We can maintain a greater degree of sanity by honestly acknowledging and learning to live with these differences in one another.

Who is trying to get you to be different than you are?

Do you allow yourself to be manipulated by him or her?

What does this person want you to be like?

How are you not like that?

Who are you trying to change from the way they are?

What is this person like and how do you want to change that?

Have you been able to change them?

Healthy boundaries define our legitimate needs and those of others, and they enable us to meet them.

We all have needs. In some respects we are given to one another to meet legitimate needs. Parents are given to their children to meet needs that only the parents are supposed to meet. Husbands and wives are given to each other to meet needs that only they are supposed to meet. We have needs relationally, spiritually, physically, sexually, and emotionally—all the areas where we have boundary issues. We need to know what our needs are and what the needs of others are in our lives.

We have problems in relationships when we fail to know what these needs are in our lives and the lives of others.

We also have problems in relationships when we look at other people's needs through our own needs. We project our needs upon other persons, assuming that they want the same things out of the relationship that we want. We need to learn to see each other from their point of need while maintaining our own individuality. Many problems in marriages today could be resolved more easily if both parties would try to look at the other's needs and begin to have a relationship based on each other's real needs.

There is a difference, however, between meeting the legitimate needs of others in our lives and feeling responsible for fixing them. It is not our place to fix other people.

Learning boundaries for ourselves should increase our awareness of other people's needs and boundaries.

List your needs as best as you can:

Put a check mark beside those needs which are your responsibility to meet.

Circle those needs that are the responsibility of someone else to meet.

Have you communicated your needs to the person who is responsible for meeting them?

Have others in your life communicated to you their needs that you are responsible for meeting?

Healthy boundaries empower us to have intimacy in relationships.
Intimacy happens when two whole, healthy persons are in touch with their feelings, thoughts, and desires and share themselves with each other in a healthy, supportive manner.

It is hard for most of us to get in touch with what we really feel, think, and desire. It is even harder to express a feeling at the time we are feeling it if we grew up being shamed for having that feeling.

If we don't know who we are, we will take on false selves. We will go out and meet another person who has taken on a false self and we'll try to be intimate with that person. People will date for a year, get married, and one of them will wake up the next morning wondering, "Who is this person I married?" It's impossible to achieve intimacy if we are not in touch with our feelings, thoughts, and desires.

Intimacy is more than having sex with another person. If we know who we are and we are married to another person who knows who he or she is, we can enjoy emotional and physical closeness. If we are close emotionally, then we can be close physically.

If intimacy means really knowing one another, then the lack of intimacy comes from not knowing one another.[1]

We may not know what our feelings are or know how to handle them, but we have them anyway. If we don't control them, they will control us. We don't know what to do with these feelings, so we medicate them with addictions and obsessive-compulsive behaviors. We find a way to deal with them.

As we come to know ourselves and our feelings, we will be able to develop emotional boundaries.

Who is the person with whom you have the most intimate relationship?

What does this person know about you that no one else knows?

How accepting is this person of you, having known these things about you?

What do you know about this person?

How accepting are you of this person?

What things are you afraid to tell this person about yourself?

Why are you afraid to tell this person these things?

Healthy boundaries bring order into our lives.
If we are undisciplined and disorderly, our lives are going to be unmanageable. We will experience frustration, perhaps depression, and feel terrible about ourselves. The reverse of this begins to happen as we are able to set healthy boundaries.

How would you rate order in your life: non-existent, poor, medium, good, great, too much of it?

To what do you attribute the disorder in your life (character defects, circumstances, relationship problems, etc.)?

What effect does this disorder have upon your life?

Healthy boundaries empower us to determine how we will be treated by others.

They define the limits and extent of how far others can go and not go in their relationships with us.

Most of us from non-nurturing families have taught people in our lives that it is OK to violate our boundaries because our boundaries are tentative and negotiable. For example, a girl tells her date, "I'm remaining celibate, and that's just out of bounds." Yet, three weeks later she calls and says, "Can we come to counseling? We're involved in a sexually active relationship here that we didn't really intend..." Her boundary was weak; her date disrespected her boundary, so she was easily seduced.

Who are you allowing to mistreat you?

How have you taught them to mistreat you this way?

What boundary do you think you should have with this person?

Why don't you have it?

How is this person manipulating his or her way past your boundaries?

Healthy boundaries empower us to have self-discipline, maturity, and strength of character.

Having healthy boundaries could very well be a definition of maturity. As we develop healthy boundaries, we automatically become more disciplined and mature. We will have strength of character that we did not have before.

Healthy boundaries help us to grow up. People in our relationships will notice this maturity and come to respect us more. They will be attracted to what they see in us and tend to receive us rather than use us. They will relate more honestly and realistically with us.

How do you see healthy boundaries contributing to self-discipline in your life?

How do you see healthy boundaries contributing to maturity in your life?

How do you see healthy boundaries contributing to strength of character in your life?

Healthy boundaries empower us to stand against manipulation.

Carrie was a long-time member of her women's club. It was time to select a delegate to the national convention, and Carrie seemed a natural choice.

"No, thank you," Carrie replied in quiet confidence, "I don't go to conventions."

"But, Carrie," argued one of the members, "you *ought* to go. We need you to represent us."

"I don't go to conventions," she insisted.

"But you've never been before," replied another member."

"I don't go to conventions."

"But it's such a beautiful resort. You will have such great time."

"I don't go to conventions."

"But you will meet lots of new people."

"I don't go to conventions."

"But Susan is going, and you know what a hoot she is."

"I don't go to conventions."

"But it's only three days..."

"I don't go to conventions."

Finally, they resolved that Carrie doesn't go to conventions. Had Carrie been uncertain who she was and what she liked, she would not have been sure whether she went to conventions or not. Even if she knew that she didn't like them, she would have been persuaded to go anyway. She would have felt ashamed of saying *no*. She would have pretended to enjoy it even if she had a miserable time. Furthermore, she would have resented them for talking her into going, but they would never have found that out.

Our Carrie, on the other hand, had a firm boundary. She knew what she liked and didn't like and what she wanted and didn't want to do. She was able to quietly and confidently stand by her position which she had every right to have. It might have been helpful for her to go, but it was not essential, and someone else could take charge of that responsibility.

Imagine yourself as Carrie in this meeting. How would you have responded to the urgings of the group?

Healthy boundaries define what we are and are not responsible for and also teach us responsibility.

Job descriptions in companies are boundaries. They define what is and is not one's job. They are standards that the company sets up to evaluate one's performance on the job. They serve as a legal description of what that person is supposed to do, when and where he is to do it, and how much he can expect to get paid for doing it.

He is then taught how to do the job. All the things he is shown about how to do his job involves boundaries. He is told what the boundaries are, and the boundaries, consequently, teach him how to do his job—what to do and what not to do.

In this same way, boundaries teach us responsibilities in all areas of life. What are our responsibilities as children growing up? What are our responsibilities to our aging parents after we grow up? What are our responsibilities to our children when they are growing up? What about after they grow up? Boundaries in these relationships change.

We violate boundaries when we fail to do the things we are supposed to do, do the things we are not supposed to do, and allow others to impose upon us what is not ours to do.

When have you been uncertain about your responsibilities (such as at home, in the marriage, at work, school, etc.)?

How has this uncertainty created a boundary problem?

Whose boundary was crossed?

How was it crossed?

Whose job is it to make your responsibilities known to you?

How would a clarification of your responsibility in that situation have changed anything?

Healthy boundaries empower us to say *no* when we need to say *no* and *yes* when we really want to say *yes*.

We need to learn to say *no* to the bad and *yes* to the good. *No* is a powerful word. It is a complete sentence. It needs no explanation. This little two-letter word can be a powerful influence in establishing boundaries and coming to know who we really are.

Children need to retain the right to say *no* regardless of how small they are. If they are allowed to say *no* when it is appropriate to do so and thereby develop a sense of boundaries for themselves as children, they will be able to carry that into adulthood. Allowing them to say *no*, however, does not mean that children should always get their way. Parents have the difficult task of balancing the freedom to say *no* with discipline. Sound discipline is also an important tool for teaching boundaries to children.

Part of learning to say *no* is learning how to accept a *no* from others.

Saying *no* is how we empower ourselves. Here are some of the powers associated with saying *no*.

YES and NO define relationships. You cannot really know who you are until you can say *no* to another. It brings wholeness and integrity into your personhood. *No* is a chisel against the shapeless rock of codependency. The more you use it, the more you chisel away what is not you and sculpt what is the true you.

NO, therefore, is a boundary that defines who you are. A solid *no* to another's abuse is a solid *yes* to your own identity as a person. Even beyond abuse, it is saying I am me. I am not you.

NO, therefore, is a positive, not a negative. It has to do with taking positive action.

NO is a right. We need to exercise our right to use it. The right to say *yes* and *no* have to do with being free—having liberty.

NO strengthens the ability to make other choices. A strengthened *no* in one area strengthens our ability to say *no* in other more difficult areas.

NO frees us to say *yes*. After you learn to say *no*, you are free to say *yes* when it is appropriate to do so.

NO involves being comfortable with yourself. Life is simpler lived when we have the confidence to say *no* when we need to say *no*.

NO strengthens character. The *no* has to come from within the inner person. It has to become who you are.

NO is a solid shield against manipulation. You don't need any further explanation or qualification. It does not have to mean *maybe*. It is a powerful tool against unwanted intrusions.

NO informs and educates the other party, teaches him or her what is acceptable and not. It teaches others how to treat us.

NO identifies ownership. This is me; this is mine; I am not you; you are not me; you cannot have this; you cannot touch this; you cannot say this; you cannot do this.

NO teaches boundaries in relationship to children. It needs to be balanced with an appropriate *yes*. No and *yes* need to be consistent, reasonable, and protective.

Who are the persons in your life to whom you need to learn to say *no*?

To what things that they ask of you do you need to say *no*?

How has your *yes* affected you when it should have been a *no*? What damage has it brought to you?

How might your life be different if you were saying an appropriate *no* to what you are now saying an inappropriate *yes*?

Based on what you have learned in this chapter, what new healthy boundaries can you begin to exercise in your relationships?

GROUP EXPERIENCE

Group Leader:

1. Ask if there are any questions about the information in this chapter. Allow others to answer through group discussion.

2. Have group members turn to a person sitting next to them, look him or her in the eye, and take turns saying, "I don't want you to treat me that way anymore." Then ask:

How did the exercise make you feel? (Uncomfortable? Silly? Anxious? Strange?)

How did it make you feel to say that?

How did it make you feel to be told that?

Was it new for you to say that?

What does that tell you about yourself and your boundaries?

3. Divide the group into pairs and ask them to share their answers from this chapter that were most significant to them. Also have them evaluate with one another the new boundaries they have decided they can begin to exercise.

4. Bring the group back together to discuss final questions, thoughts, and feelings before leaving.

Set time limits on these group sessions. Remind participants that they do not have to share anything they are not ready to share.

– 4 –

Characteristics of Persons
with Healthy Boundaries

*P*ersons with healthy boundaries are those who have a clear sense of themselves. They know their strengths and weaknesses, what they want, don't want, like, dislike, etc., and are OK with themselves. Furthermore, they have a fairly clear sense of who others are and are OK with them. This does not mean that they live off in La-la Land and never have crises. It does mean that they have the inner resources to deal with these crises. Here are some of the characteristics of persons with healthy boundaries.

Persons with healthy boundaries are secure within themselves.

They are not threatened by others who are different from themselves or who have a different view from theirs. They are open enough to admit new ideas and perspectives while preserving their individuality.[1]

Persons with healthy boundaries do not allow themselves to be intruded upon.

This does not mean that they build up a wall around themselves. Healthy boundaries are not walls. Walls, in the natural sense, may delineate a boundary like the Great Wall of China or the Berlin Wall—they are defenses. They are designed to keep things in or out. If we don't have healthy boundaries, we have defenses. But healthy boundaries cannot be walls in a relationship. Healthy boundaries are more like gates that latch from the inside, putting the gatekeepers in charge of who and what they allow in or keep out.

Most of us have opened ourselves up to inappropriate people who have hurt us. We reacted by isolating ourselves. Isolating is a type of wall we put up between us and other hurtful people. When our walls go up, they not only keep out the intruder, but everybody else as well.

Persons with healthy boundaries are those who have a clear sense of their own views, values, and priorities.

When we fail to know what our values and priorities are, we are going to allow others to determine them for us. Elected political officials are supposed to represent the views of their constituents. This is accomplished by different candidates setting forth their own views, values, and priorities. The general populous then votes for the one they believe best represents their views, values, and priorities. If that official does not have healthy boundaries concerning his views, values, and priorities, he will change with every whim.

Persons with healthy boundaries are able to discern safe and appropriate people with whom to disclose things about themselves.

When we openly tell things about ourselves to unsafe people, we run the risk of being violated by them. We want to be careful to whom we bare our souls.

Those of us who have experienced rejection from caregivers look for approval from people who are not going to give it to us. We have been doing that all of our lives because Mom and Dad never gave it to us. Ironically, the more they didn't give it to us, the more we tried to get it from them. This compulsion to gain approval from people who won't give it to us continues into adult life. We take ourselves and our little project to other people, and they spit up all over it. This feeds our shame and reinforces our deepest fears: "I told you that you were a no-good trash-bag." Without healthy boundaries in relationships, we will continue to live out these self-fulfilling prophecies.

Persons with healthy boundaries have enough confidence in themselves that they are little affected by the mean things others can say or do to them.

These people are not sterile of feelings. No one is. But when mean things are done to persons with healthy boundaries, they are able to withstand the attack and process their feelings. People with unhealthy boundaries are defenseless against the attack and usually stuff their feelings.

As long as we live as conscious human beings in this world, we are going to be in relationships. As long as we are in relationships, we will hurt others and be hurt by others to one degree or another. We have a choice in what we do with the pain.

Not everyone who hurts us intends to do so. People don't always deliberately do things to us, they just do things. Healthy boundaries can help us to deal with those hurtful people as well as teach us how to protect ourselves from them.

Nevertheless, we don't have to isolate to stay protected. We can learn to stand up to the attack by practicing healthy boundaries and taking charge of our lives. It may produce anxiety at first, but we can learn how to take responsibility for ourselves and say *no* to abuse.

Persons with healthy boundaries can protect themselves without imprisoning themselves.

If we resort to building walls and hiding behind them, we only imprison ourselves. With healthy boundaries we can safely move in and out of relationships at will. But walls don't allow us to go in and out.

Persons with healthy boundaries know how to assert themselves at appropriate times in order to stay out of the victim role.

If we are living out of shame, we will live in fear of conflict. If we live in fear of conflict, we are more likely to live in isolation. If we can't isolate, we will do whatever we can to avoid conflict.

We may get into the volunteer victim role and stay there for years until we can't stand it anymore—then we blow a fuse. We go nuclear and blast everybody out and smash the plates in the kitchen. When we realize what we've done, it's "Oh my, that was horrible. I'm so ashamed of myself. I'm so sorry." Even though we had a right to assert ourselves, we waited until the feelings built up and had an edge on them.

Victim　　　　　　　Assertion　　　　　　　Aggression

We went from victim to aggression and skipped over assertion, which means we're the one who's wrong—once again. Now, we go back all hang-dogged saying, "I'm sor-r-ry." We end up making the apology instead of the one who victimized us.

So we set ourselves up to move back into the victim role. We'll stay there until we get emotionally charged again. We develop a backlog of resentment toward our mates, kids, boss, or others, and we haven't had the strength to tell them what's going on with us. So, it comes out on an unsuspecting, innocent check-out clerk at the supermarket. The clerk says, "Can I see your driver's license?"

"What do you mean, 'see my driver's license'? I've got money! I'm so sick of you people asking to see my driver's license I could blow up!"

It's not about the driver's license; it's about displaced anger because we don't know about assertion. Assertion requires setting boundaries:

"I thought I told you I didn't like that."

"Excuse me, you did that again and we've talked about this before and maybe I need to tell you again, 'don't do that, I don't like it.'"

"That makes me feel sad."

"That makes me feel angry."

"When you do that, it hurts my feelings."

"Don't say that to me."

"Maybe I am oversensitive, but I can't help it right now."

Those are assertive kinds of things to say.

Persons with healthy boundaries are able to enter into relationships with others without losing themselves.

"I am not you." That is a profound statement worthy of repeating until we get the point. If we can grasp that reality, we will have made phenomenal progress in our recovery from abuses. We get to be who we are and make these external connections without fear of losing our identity.

Codependents are so preoccupied with others that they sacrifice their own values, wants, and needs. They wake up in the morning, walk out the door, stop the first person they see, and say, "How am I feeling?" That person promptly tells them, and the codependents go around the rest of the day acting out what was told them by another. "You're feeling lousy."

"Thank you very much, I knew something was wrong." For codependents there is no definition of who they are.

We can start with, "I don't know who I am, but I know I'm not you. I'm not my husband, I'm not my wife, I'm not my daddy, I'm not my mama, and I'm not my brother. I'm not my boss, and I'm not my fellow worker. I'm me. Who 'me' is, I don't know yet." We may not be that far into our recovery, but to recognize those facts is a start.

Answer the following questions by circling the number that you think is most accurate for you. This evaluation is not intended to make you feel like an awful person, but to help you break through denial and see reality. Also, these kinds of questions cause you to see how boundaries apply to many areas of your life that you have not thought of before. It, thereby, serves to teach you more about boundaries.

	None 1	Little 2	Average 3	Much 4	Always 5
How much are you threatened by others whose moral views are different from yours?	1	2	3	4	5
How much are you threatened by others whose political views are different from yours?	1	2	3	4	5
How much are you threatened by others whose religious views are different from yours?	1	2	3	4	5
How much do you allow yourself and your views to be run over by intrusive people?	1	2	3	4	5
How much do you allow others to determine your values for you?	1	2	3	4	5
How much do you allow others to set your priorities for you?	1	2	3	4	5
How often do you tell things about yourself to the wrong people?	1	2	3	4	5
How much are you thrown off base by people who say and do ugly things to you?	1	2	3	4	5
How much do you throw up a wall to protect yourself from others' abuses?	1	2	3	4	5

How often do you store up feelings until they
explode and then feel you must apologize for
the explosion?   1   2   3   4   5

How much do you allow yourself to become lost
in the other persons with whom you choose to
connect?   1   2   3   4   5

An answer of "none" indicates a strong, healthy boundary. An answer of "always" indicates a weak, unhealthy boundary or no boundary at all. Based on your answers, would you say that you have boundaries that are mostly excellent, good, fair, poor, or non-existent?

Based on what you have learned in this chapter, what new healthy boundaries can you begin to exercise in your relationships?

GROUP EXPERIENCE

Group Leader:

1. Ask if there are any questions about the information in this chapter. Allow others to answer through group discussion.

2. Ask if anyone wants to tell about a personal experience that illustrates any of the points made in this chapter.

3. Divide the group into pairs and ask them to share their answers to the preceding list of questions. Also have them tell how they are doing with any new boundaries that they have begun to exercise and evaluate with one another any additional boundaries they have decided to set.

4. Bring the group back together to discuss final questions, thoughts, and feelings before leaving.

Set time limits on these group sessions. Remind participants that they do not have to share anything they are not ready to share.

— 5 —

Where We Learn Boundaries

---

*T*he first three years of a child's life are very crucial to the development of boundaries. Boundaries are experienced from the moment of birth. These early years are the time when children learn the difference between what is "me" and what is "not me." They first learn boundaries from their family of origin—hopefully, they learn healthy boundaries through proper parental discipline.

Child psychologists have identified four major developmental stages that occur in a child's life during these early years. These have a direct bearing upon boundary development.

DEVELOPMENTAL STAGES

The first stage in a child's life has been called symbiotic.

Biologically speaking, symbiosis is the intimate living together of two kinds of organisms, especially where such association is of mutual advantage. Since the child in the womb is one with his mother and is totally dependent upon his mother for life, it is appropriate to say it is a symbiotic relationship.

After birth, he still doesn't know that he and mom are not one and the same. His mother's boundary is his boundary. His experience is saying, "I am you."

No one can calm him like his own mother during this period. He knows his mother's touch, voice, smell, and vibrations. Months and years later he will run to mama for consolation, safety, and reassurance when he gets hurt or offended. Mama's touch, voice, smell, and vibrations are essential for establishing the boundaries that define his identity.

Dad and other family members enter this picture soon after birth. They are the child's first contact with the world. Much of what happens within those first days dictates the kind of life he will experience for the rest of his life.

Babies are totally dependent upon their caregivers to meet their every physical need. They need the consistent and predictable emotional support that comes from being held and cared for by loving hands.

This is the time for children to properly bond with others in their lives if they are to pass on to other developmental stages. Failure of parents to allow healthy bonding during this time can send a message that they are rejected, unwanted, and unattached—a feeling that can be carried into adult life and cause boundary problems.

The second stage in a child's development is called individuation, or hatching.

This is a time of separation. Cuddly little Susie has now turned into a barn-buster. An internal alarm goes off that tells her it's time to start separating from Mom and gain some autonomy. She is beginning to sense that she is not her mother. Her experience is now saying, "I am me."

Children develop a sense of "mine" during this time. They are learning their limits. They are in a zone between total dependence and attempts at independence which come later on.

Holding and touching are important to this process of individuation. Holding and touching are ways of confirming with the hands that the child is no longer attached to Mom but is an entity who exists outside of her. It also conveys to the child that she is loved and wanted. This is very important to the development of healthy boundaries.

The third stage in a child's development is called practicing and rides on the heels of individuation.

Children in this stage are practicing independence. They not only separate themselves from Mom, but take on an attitude that says, "Get out of my way. Can't you see? I can do anything." They turn further away from dependency on Mom to explore that vast and wonderful world of cabinet doorknobs, light plugs, and big brother's stuffed animals. They have gone from "I am you" to "I am me" and on to "mine."

This is the time children learn that most important, yet dreadful two-letter word, *NO!* The parent who doesn't know what is going on during this time will imprint the children with negative mental impressions of themselves. "Don't you tell me 'no' you stinking little brat." "Don't you say 'no' to your mother." "You're a bad kid. I don't know what we are going to do with you." *No* is their word for everything, even when they mean *yes*. Later on, stifled adult children of dysfunction have to join a codependency group just to learn that it is OK to say *no*.

Children in this stage cannot understand the difference between the *no* of a tantrum and the *no* of a boundary. They have to be taught this difference through a program of healthy discipline. They need to learn what is safe and healthy behavior and what is not. It's the parents' job to teach them this difference. Failure of the parents to teach children this difference leaves them with a foggy sense of boundaries. Parents need to set limits for their children that will cause them to develop healthy boundaries while, at the same time, allowing them enough slack to emerge into the unique persons God intended.

In their book, *Boundaries*, Henry Cloud and John Townsend define discipline as "an external boundary designed to develop internal boundaries in our children." They make a distinction between discipline and punishment. "Punishment," they write, "is payment for wrongdoing." Discipline is "the natural law of God [whereby] our actions reap consequences." Punishment looks back while discipline looks forward.[1] Children need to be taught boundaries. They need to know what the foul lines are. They also need to know what the consequences are for violating boundaries. They will test their limits to see how far they can go before the parents say *no.* They feel secure when their parents and other caretakers create safe limits for them.

In addition to learning what the boundaries of others are, children need also to be given a sense of their own boundaries. They need to have their own boundaries respected. They will learn healthy boundaries by the respect they are shown by their caregivers.

The fourth stage in a child's development is called interdependence.

Children in this stage learn that they are in community and have, after all, a need to be connected. They begin to re-establish cordial relationships with others in their family. Their experience is saying, "I am me, you are you, and we need each other in our separateness."

Healthy children are allowed to progress from dependence, to individuation, to practicing, to interdependence. When they return to mom, they do so with a clearer sense of who they are as separate from her. "I am *me,* but I still need you."

By the time children pass through these first three years, "they should have mastered the following tasks," write Cloud and Townsend:

1. The ability to be emotionally attached to others, yet without giving up a sense of self and one's freedom to be apart.
2. The ability to say appropriate *no's* to others without fear of loss of love.
3. The ability to take appropriate *no's* from others without withdrawing emotionally.[2]

While boundaries continue to be built throughout our lives, most of them are established during these formative years.

Those early abusive childhood experiences are the ones that injure the most. The kind of boundaries that we are taught during those first four developmental stages set off patterns that repeat themselves throughout our lives unless we do something deliberately to alter them. Counselor John Bradshaw says that we replay these childhood stages of development in every new relationship.

We can only have relationships in the way we know how to have them. Codependents think, "The old relationship is the problem. I'll divorce this guy and get a new guy, and I'll have a new relationship." Wrong! We won't. We won't have new ways of having relationships until we learn new ways of having relationships.

It takes years to go through the stages of development to achieve intimacy. We have to unlearn the things we wrongly experienced as a child and learn the things we should have learned during these developmental years. We have to go back to see how we were incorrectly printed. If we suffered from a lost childhood, we will still have a lost child within us. We have to go through the stages of grief over that lost childhood in order to get past it.

MARY BETH'S STORY

Memories may begin in the womb. With two babies ages one and two, Mary Beth's mother was not prepared to be pregnant again. Mary Beth later recalled feelings of being unwanted and of being a burden and was very still in the womb. Her parents thought something might be wrong with her. But Mary Beth possibly was meeting her mother's need even before she was born by being quiet and good.

In early infancy, she slept so much they often had to wake her up to feed her. Seemingly the "easy" child, she grew up under the impression, "I have to be good in order to be loved." She experienced distress, depression and fear. She felt that she was not a problem when she was sucking her thumb, and comforted herself that way. Mary Beth survived these feelings by becoming a lost child—the quiet one who never caused trouble and stayed out of the way.

Her mother's father died two weeks before she was born, and she remembers her mother being sad. She was a comfort to her mother in the midst of this loss. As Mary Beth learned to meet her mother's emotional needs, she became more compliant and less mindful of her own needs, thus more co-dependent.

These dynamics plus the need for male attention in Mary Beth's childhood were early setups for her to be vulnerable to improper advances from her sixth-grade science teacher. He wrote her notes and slipped them to her as she was getting on the school bus. "Don't tell the other teachers," he warned. He wrote things about her eyes and about wishing she sat closer to the front of the class. When Mary Beth found out that he was doing the same thing to other girls, she was confused and didn't know what to think or feel.

In the eighth grade, her guidance counselor invited her to work for him during her study hall. That sounded great to a junior high student. She got out of study hall to help him with grades and schedules. It was fun at first, but he slowly and gradually desensitized her and manipulated her emotions with his inappropriate comments, notes, and attention. He continued to cross one boundary after another until eventually it became sexual abuse.

Two years of dealing with the relationship was making Mary Beth crazy. She was not enjoying the normal childhood that her friends were having. It seemed to help when she finally told a girl friend what was going on. She tried to put a stop to the relationship, but she had become very emotionally dependent upon this man. She schemed a way to try to see him again and found him with another girl. She felt devastated and totally betrayed. Not only had she suffered from emotional and sexual abuse, now she had to deal with the abuse of rejection.

She was damaged a long time by that relationship. With no outside help for her problem, she remained vulnerable and attracted to other boundary violators creating a destructive cycle of unhealthy relationships in her life. She had gone on to college and was relieved to get away, but ended up having inappropriate relationships with two of her professors. She only weighed 85 to 90 pounds, not because she had an eating disorder but because she had an emotional disorder. We are as sick as our secrets.

In an attempt to escape the insanity of these affairs, she moved to another state and took a job working in a rehab program. After many lonely months she agreed to go out with a graduate of this program, an ex-heroin addict. Six months later they were married.

Mary Beth had no first-hand experience dealing with an addict. The program where she worked was so behavior modification oriented that she had not learned the crucial information she needed about the diseases of chemical dependency or codependency. Within a month after their marriage, her husband was totally strung out again on heroin. He stole all of the money they had and began to pawn things, including items that she cherished.

Months later she returned home to her parents emotionally disabled. She was unable to work or do anything for the better part of a year. Finding herself spiritually, mentally, emotionally, and physically sick, she finally hit bottom and asked for help.

As she discovered her lack of boundaries, she began to establish new, strong ones. However, her fear of repeating past mistakes caused her boundaries to become inflexible even when it was appropriate to make an exception. Her recovery still involves the process of establishing and maintaining healthy boundaries that are neither too rigid or too loose.

List the cast of characters in Mary Beth's story and briefly describe your impressions of each.

What relationships would you write into Mary Beth's story to alter these tragic events in her life? At what stage of her life would you write them in?

Who are you most like in this story and how?

THE FAMILY SYSTEM

A family is a system, a unit, that is made up of several parts which are related and connected. We grow up in systems. We cannot exist outside of a system. Churches, schools, commerce, government, and societies are all systems.

One of the ways we can look at the family system is to think of it as a mobile where each family member is hanging like a puppet on one of the strings. Imagine something coming through and rocking one member of the family which will automatically cause all the other members of the family to be affected. Each member will adjust himself or herself to create some sort of balance, or they may all continue to rock for a while.

In a healthy family system each person contributes something to make it work smoothly and to meet the needs of each member. If a member is unable to do his job, the system gets out of balance and somebody else has to take up the slack. If mom gets sick and has to go to the hospital, different members of the family pitch in to make up for her absence. Dad takes care of the meals, the son does the laundry, and the older daughter helps the younger daughter get ready for school. When mom gets well and things get back to normal, the whole family moves back in balance. There is a cooperative effort to keep the system functioning as well as possible.

No matter what's going on in the family, the family system will always try to achieve balance, just as a mobile does.

Briefly describe a major event that rocked the balance of your family of origin when you were growing up. Tell what you remember and/or what you were told about the occurrence.

How did the family respond?

What effect did that event have upon other members of the family?

What effect do you think it might have had upon you?

GROWING UP IN A FUNCTIONAL FAMILY

For the purposes of our study, we are classifying families as functional (nurturing) or dysfunctional (non-nurturing) systems. Functional simply means it works! The ideal functional family is a partnership led by a healthy father. The absence of either parent renders the family dysfunctional to one degree or another. A functional family is characterized by the existence of healthy, functional boundaries.

In functional families, the parents are able to meet their own needs and those of their children.

Healthy families have rules that stimulate personal growth. The rules are fair, realistic, clearly identifiable, consistent, predictable, and edifying.

Healthy family members communicate with themselves and others openly and honestly. They discuss family problems together. It's OK to have feelings and to express those feelings without abusive repercussions. It's OK to be angry, cry, make mistakes, feel pain, and laugh.

It's OK to play. It's OK to have needs. It's OK to have privacy. It's OK to have personal things and to share them. It's OK to trust others and yourself.

Healthy family members accept responsibility when they are wrong and are able to ask forgiveness and to forgive.

They give each other permission to be themselves. They have respect for individuality and provide support for growth.

Functional family members are comfortable with their own bodies and have a healthy sexual outlook. This is the "Leave It To Beaver" Cleaver family album. It is hardly the picture we see thumbing through our family-of-origin albums.

GROWING UP IN A DYSFUNCTIONAL FAMILY

Dysfunctional simply means it doesn't work, but it often looks like it does. In contrast to a functional family, it has been suggested that the dysfunctional family is a dictatorship run by its sickest member. It is one that does not function in a normal, healthy way. The family members are unable to find stability. A dysfunctional family is characterized by a lack of boundaries.

We usually think of alcoholism or drug addiction in the family as the primary cause of the dysfunction, but it can also be caused by a variety of other different problems that families face: a serious illness (such as cancer), a death in the family, or mental illness. It can be caused by either an extramarital affair, religious abuse, or other abuses. It can be caused by anything that rocks or stresses the family.

The question is no longer, "Did I come from a dysfunctional family?" but "To what degree was my family dysfunctional?"

It is not "How dysfunctional was my family?" but "In what ways was it dysfunctional?"

It is not "Did it affect me to come from this family?" but "How did it affect me, what roles did I play, and what am I left with now?"

It is not "Do I need to do something about my family of origin and the resulting boundary issues?" but "What do I do to address the specific issues resulting from my dysfunctional family of origin?"

DYSFUNCTIONAL FAMILY ROLES

In an effort to survive and to find some stability in an unstable, stressful environment, the family members develop survival roles. A survival role is basically a pattern of defenses that each family member adopts to give him or her the least amount of personal stress.

As you read about the classic roles you will see yourself in one of these roles to one degree or another.[3] If you were an only child, you may have played all the roles. If things changed in your family, you may have changed roles. As you read about the survival roles, think about which one(s) you most closely identify with. Think about other members of your family of origin and how they fit these roles.

The addict

Anyone in the family can play this role, but we usually think of it as the mother or father. In our classic model of a dysfunctional family, we identify the father as the addict, perhaps an alcoholic. He is the root cause for the family to be dysfunctional. He is very dependent and is always shifting the blame on someone or something else.

He has repressed feelings of pain, guilt, shame, fear, and anger.

He is out of touch with reality and hides behind walls of anger, denial, charm, projection, rigidity, aggressiveness, hostility, self-righteousness, high standards for others, grandiosity, over-achievement, blaming, and perfectionism.

He medicates his pain and bad feelings with some addictive substance or behavior that becomes debilitating (for example, overeating, gambling, or sex). His medicator is used to relieve his pain but does nothing to relieve the pain of the family. He will compulsively use people, places, or things.

Who was the addict in your family of origin?

What was the addict's addiction (drug of choice)?

Who is the addict in your present family?

What is his/her addiction (drug of choice)?

The chief enabler

The chief enabler is usually the mother in our classic model of an alcoholic home. She is the one who is closest and most depended upon by the addict. She enables him in his disease by doing things like calling his work and telling them he's sick when he's really drunk. She enables the disease to progress by doing things for the addict that he should be doing for himself. As the addict increasingly loses control, the chief enabler makes more of the decisions and takes on more responsibility.

She is codependent which means that she depends upon the addict to justify her need to be a caretaker. Melody Beattie in *Codependent No More* gives this definition, "A codependent person is one who has let another person's behavior affect him or her, and who is obsessed with controlling that person's behavior."4 She develops dependence upon the other person (or thing) to the point of neglecting herself.

Characteristically, she is super-responsible. She wears a masked smile, pretending that everything is "fine." Yet, she has repressed feelings of hurt, anger, emptiness, guilt, and inadequacy. She feels stuck, overwhelmed, and powerless.

She hides behind walls of martyrdom, seriousness, control, denial, people-pleasing, caretaking, protecting, rescuing, over-responsibility, self-blaming, hostility, low self-worth, physical illnesses, and fragility.

Caretaking makes the chief enabler feel important and self-righteous. The family benefits because someone is taking responsibility for things in the home. She will pay the price for her caretaking with physical or emotional illness. Her primary compulsion is to take charge. She is a control addict.

Who was the chief enabler in your family of origin?

Who is the chief enabler in your present family?

The hero

The family hero is usually the oldest child. He (or she), too, is super-responsible. He not only takes responsibility off his mom's shoulders, but does his best to make good grades, make the team, work an extra job—whatever it takes to make the family look good. He provides a sense of worth for the family. He takes on a lot of the responsibility that the enabling spouse cannot fulfill because she is busy taking care of the addict.

He has repressed feelings of guilt, inadequacy, loneliness, confusion, anger, and hurt.

He hides behind walls of trying to be someone special, people-pleasing, helpfulness, approval-seeking, over-achieving, intellectualizing, being the little parent. He gets a lot of attention and acclaim. He is compulsive and driven and becomes a workaholic. It is not uncommon for the hero to become the addict later on in life.

Who was the hero in your family of origin?

Who is the hero in your present family?

The scapegoat

The scapegoat is often the second child. His (or her) own rebelliousness takes the focus away from the addicted person. He has a very strong peer alliance outside of the home because he doesn't feel like he belongs in the family. He carries the pain of the family which is why he is given the name scapegoat. He gets blamed for the problems in the family even though his behavior is the result, not the cause of dysfunction. The addict is the problem in the family. The scapegoat often gets in trouble with the law doing things on purpose or subconsciously to get out of the family.

He has repressed feelings of insecurity, anger, hurt, rejection, fear, and loneliness.

He hides behind walls of rebelliousness, defiance, blaming, acting out, trouble-making, peer preference over family, chemical abuse, getting arrested and going to prison, and withdrawing. If the scapegoat is a female, her acting out may result in an unplanned pregnancy. The scapegoat is a low achiever and high risk for suicide.

Who was the scapegoat in your family of origin?

Who is the scapegoat in your present family?

The lost child

The lost child may be the middle child in the family. She (or he) is typically sweet, quiet, and shy. She is the child the family doesn't have to worry about. She offers the family relief. She learns not to rock the boat. She tends to stay in her little fantasy world and often ends up with a lot of emotional problems. She can be very manipulative and have trouble making decisions, but can be very creative in the arts.

She will have repressed feelings of being ignored, confusion, hurt, inadequacy, unimportance, and anger.

She hides behind walls of being quiet, withdrawn, and invisible; of being a loner, dreamer, and super-independent; of avoiding stressful situations; of low-achievement; of asthma, bed-wetting, eating disorders, confused sexual identity, and promiscuous behavior.

Who was the lost child in your family of origin?

Who is the lost child in your present family?

The mascot

The mascots are usually the youngest children in the family. They provide the comic relief from stress for the family. They learn that things get a little easier around the house when they act cute. They are often immature and are not taken seriously. The family regards them as fragile and in need of protection. Mascots discover that being cute or funny relieves tension around the house and helps them to get in the spotlight occasionally.

They have repressed feelings of being crazy, being scared, high anxiety, hurt, loneliness, confusion, and pain.

They hide behind walls of providing distraction, being gutsy, feeling special, having pets, seeking attention, and clowning around. They are hyperactive, fragile, compulsive givers, and can't handle stress.

Who was the mascot in your family of origin?

Who is the mascot in your present family?

DYSFUNCTIONAL FAMILY RULES

In addition to establishing survival roles, dysfunctional families also develop unhealthy rules within the family system. These unhealthy rules stifle personal growth. They are unrealistic, debilitating, and are always changing so that the members can never get it right. These rules are more non-verbal than verbal, subconscious than conscious.

Some examples of unhealthy family rules are
- Don't talk; keep secrets; never talk about it.
- Don't feel; don't express feelings; stay out of touch with feelings; internalize feelings.
- Don't trust; don't expect accountability.
- Shift blame on others; deny, deny, deny; never accept responsibility.
- Pretend everything is fine; play it safe; make us proud.
- Always stay in control; be strong, good, right, perfect; act like the perfect family; go to church.
- Do what is right (even though what is right always changes).
- Don't be selfish; it's not OK to have needs.
- Do as I say, not as I do.
- Don't rock the boat.
- Don't talk back; Dad's always right.
- Speak when spoken to.

What were the unspoken rules in your family of origin growing up?

What are the unspoken rules in your present family?

SUMMARY

Poor boundaries, therefore, are learned as the result of such things as
- parenting with too strict rules and limits;
- parenting with a lack of rules and limits;
- parenting with double standards—unreasonably different rules and limits for different family members;
- traumatic experiences (emotional, physical, sexual abuse; accidents; debilitating illness; parental death; divorce; poverty; crime); and
- being rescued from consequences.

We didn't just wake up one morning having boundary problems in our relationships with other people. There are reasons why we are the way we are and do the things we do. These reasons existed long before we did. Our boundary issues, addiction tendencies, codependency, obsessive/compulsive behaviors run in the family.

Patterns develop in our families and repeat themselves—coming from our ancestors down to parents, brothers and sisters, aunts, uncles, cousins, etc. These patterns may not show up in every member of the family, but they may be found in several members of the family through the generations. More information on and an exercise for tracking the generational patterns is found in our manual titled *The Church As a Healing Community.*[5]

Children growing up in a dysfunctional family do not know what they feel, how to think, how to behave, how to make good choices, how to relate to others, how to eat properly, exercise wisely, or how to take care of themselves. Recovery from dysfunctional family life issues involves work in all of these areas.

Write a brief summary of what you have learned about yourself as a result of answering the questions in this chapter. What thoughts and feelings do you have?

Based on what you have learned in this chapter, what new healthy boundaries can you begin to exercise in your relationships?

❦ ❦ ❦

GROUP EXPERIENCE

Group Leader:
1. Ask if there are any questions about the information in this chapter. Allow others to answer through group discussion.

2. Ask someone to share his or her list of characters in Mary Beth's story. Write these on a board if one is available.
Ask the group to identify in their own words the kinds of boundary problems these different characters had in this story.
Ask the group to suggest a rewrite of this story which would include relationships at appropriate times in Mary Beth's life to alter the tragic events of her life.

3. Ask the group to form triads and ask them to tell each other what roles each of them played in their family growing up and who played the other roles in their families.
Ask them to pick one family rule that stood out the most in their lives growing up and tell what that was.

4. Divide the group into pairs and ask them to share what they wrote in their brief summary at the end of the chapter. Also have them tell how they are doing with any new boundaries that they have begun to exercise and evaluate with one another any additional boundaries they have decided to set.

5. Bring the group back together for final questions, thoughts, and feelings that may need to be discussed before leaving.

Set time limits on these group sessions. Remind them that they do not have to share anything they are not ready to share.

— 6 —

Consequences of Growing Up in a Dysfunctional Family

*W*e suffer from several consequences when we have grown up in a dysfunctional family and have not been taught healthy boundaries. Not all of these consequences will necessarily apply to everyone. Answer the questions that apply to you personally.

We may be unable to defend ourselves when we are being abused.

When we grow up in a family or system with poor boundaries, we don't learn what is and what is not offensive behavior. Moreover, our emotions don't tell us to be offended because we are out of touch with them. When we're out of touch with our emotions, we don't know who we are or what our needs are, and so we are unaware that our needs are not being met. Our abuse meter is defective, and we don't know to defend ourselves.

Who do you think is abusing you or controlling your life in ways that you feel defenseless to stop, and how are they doing so?

We may give others too much power in our lives or we assume too much power in other's lives.

Who is trying to have more power over you than they are supposed to have?

How have you given them that power?

Over whom are you trying to exercise more power than you are supposed to have?

We may become unable to distinguish our own extreme or inappropriate behavior.

Our abuse meter doesn't know when we are being abused or when we are being abusive. We allow others to do things and say things to us that are abusive, and we don't know that they are inappropriate. These things feel normal to us because that is the way we grew up. Consequently, we grow up doing and saying these same kinds of abusive things to others, and we don't know that we are being inappropriate.

These verbal behaviors include crude teasing, foul language, criticism, gossip, yelling, name-calling, etc.

How have you recently acted inappropriately?

What would have been appropriate behavior on your part?

Our own emotional needs were not met.

In dysfunctional families, the focus is upon the addict in the family at the expense of everyone else's feelings and needs. Children suffer the most. They exist to meet the needs of the parents rather than the parents being there to meet the needs of the children.

How do you remember being touched, cuddled, made to feel secure, and allowed to play and do child-like things?

We may have become responsible for our parents or other family members resulting in a loss of our own childhood.

We grow up feeling over-responsible for others in areas inappropriate to our age and role as a child; thus we become caretakers. As a result, we have an overall feeling that we exist to meet the needs of others before we meet our own needs.

This is classic codependency. We can know we are being unhealthy caretakers when we are destroying ourselves in the process of trying to build someone else up. If we are neglecting our own needs in order to take care of the needs of someone else, then we are over the line. We have to be emotionally, mentally, physically, and spiritually healthy ourselves before we can be of much use to anybody else.

Who do you feel responsible for at the expense of your own well-being? Explain:

We usually end up denying ourselves of our own basic needs.
If we were not properly taken care of as a child, we're not likely to take care of ourselves as adults.

What basic needs of yours were neglected as you were growing up?

Which of your needs do you neglect now?

Do you eat regular or healthy meals?

Do you get sufficient sleep?

Do you rest when you are tired?

Do you have too little or too much alone time?

Do you engage in too few or too many recreational (fun) activities?

Do you engage in too little or too much exercise?

Do you push yourself beyond your limits?

Do you put in far too many hours at work?

Do you do too much for others?

We may have a distorted world view, potentially, for the rest of our lives unless we get help.

How did your childhood experiences influence your world view (other people, authorities, God, religion, parenting, etc.)?

We become vulnerable to whatever will keep those feelings contained.
This is where addictions begin to set in. Our addictions medicate these contained feelings. We avoid ourselves by the abusive use of alcohol, drugs, nicotine, sugar, caffeine; by bingeing or starving; by exercise, work, shopping, TV, sports, etc.

What substance(s) or compulsive behaviors do you use or engage in to keep your mind off your feelings?

We have insufficient contact with people who truly care about us.
One of the main characteristics of alcoholism, as with other addictions, is isolation. We isolate ourselves from the very people who can and want to help us. The last thing we will do when we are in a crisis is call our friend, pastor, sponsor, or go to a support group meeting. "I can't do that—I've got to figure this out and get well, and then I'll call him—as soon as I can get OK enough to share happy, joyous things or share the victory over this terrible time that I'm having."

How and when do you withdraw from the people who are closest to you and show the most care for you?

We grow up without a sense of self.
We become someone we are not. We get lost in the identity of someone else. That person's attitudes and behaviors dictate how we talk and act. "Have you got it together? Good. I'll join your deal." "What are we like? Oh, is that

what we are like? Oh, OK, I'll be like that. I don't like being like that but I'll be like that anyway." We deny ourselves the right to be our own person. We're out of touch with our feelings and preferences.

What are some things that you have done or presently do to be accepted or avoid the fear of rejection?

We may deny self by pretending to agree when we disagree.
We conceal our true feelings, we go along with an activity that we really don't want to do, and we never state our preference. If we do have a preference, we won't say what is even when asked. We go along with the crowd.

Tell how you have recently disagreed with another but didn't express your own opinion?

Why did you not express your own opinion?

We may decline to do things we really want to do for fear that we won't do it right.
For example, though we may like a certain athletic activity, we won't join in because our expectations of ourselves are so high that we fear failure. So we sit on the sidelines.

What have you declined to do that you really wanted to do?

Why did you not do it?

If you had it to do over, what would you do?

We may grow up hurting other people.

We either pass the hurt back or pass it on. If we pass it on, we will continue to hurt ourselves and others. We may not mean to hurt others, but we hurt them anyway. We hurt them in all of the life areas we have identified in this workbook (relationally, spiritually, physically, sexually, and emotionally).

If, on the other hand, we are able to set healthy boundaries, it is usually because we found ways to go through the pain and resolve the losses associated with the abuse. In so doing, we were able to pass the hurt back to those who passed it on to us. This involves forgiveness and not vindictiveness. When we pass it back, we are saying, "This is the end of the line. The abuse pattern ends here. I do not receive the hurt any longer." This process gives us back our power.

You will find exercises in Chapters 16 and 17 that are intended to help you come to this resolve.

How have you hurt others the way you were hurt?

Did you realize you were hurting them?

Did you realize you were hurting them in the same way you had been hurt?

We may grow up feeling unsafe.

What things, circumstances, or situations make you feel unsafe?   Why?

What are some of the things you do or did to feel safe?

We grow up with rage.

The abuses in our lives leave us with losses. We were discounted, invalidated, and not verified as human beings. So there are losses which threaten our self-hood. Those losses cause us pain. We need something strong enough to keep us out of the pain of the losses. The only emotion strong enough to do that is rage. We don't "feel" rageful, because we have been told we are not supposed to be angry, just grateful. So we suppress it. Nevertheless, the anger is deep within us in the form of rage.

Who was the angry person in your life growing up?

What do you think they were angry about?

How did they express their anger?

How did others react to their anger?

Who is the angry person in your life today?

What do you think they are angry about?

How do you react to their anger?

Do you consider yourself an angry person?

What do you do with your anger?

Who told you it was not OK to be angry?

What are you angry about?

We learn to expect little from others but expect perfection from ourselves.

Perfectionism is another device we use to further shame ourselves. We put more on ourselves than we are able to perform. Then, when we fail, we prove just how shameful we are. It's OK for others to miss the mark, but it's not OK for us.

It was not OK for us to make mistakes in our dysfunctional family of origin. If we did make a mistake, we dared not get caught. If by chance we did get caught, we blamed someone or something else. We wouldn't ever take responsibility for it; if we did, we wouldn't be perfect.

But blaming someone else for how we are will not solve anything. Regardless of how we got to be who we are, we are who we are, and we are responsible to do something about it. If we don't admit that we aren't perfect, how will we ever be in a position to do something about it? And if we don't do something about it, nobody will.

Are you a perfectionist?

What do you think about yourself when you fail to measure up to your own expectations?

What expectations have you put upon yourself?

How unrealistic do you now think these expectations are?

Other consequences

The above listing is not all inclusive of the consequences of growing up in a dysfunctional family.

What other consequences of growing up in a dysfunctional family can you think of that are not mentioned in this chapter?

Write a brief impression of what you learned about yourself as a result of answering these questions. What thoughts, feelings, and attitudes surfaced or became more clear to you?

Based on what you have learned in this chapter, what new healthy boundaries can you begin to exercise in your relationships?

GROUP EXPERIENCE

Group Leader:
1. Ask if there are any questions about the information in this chapter. Allow others to answer through group discussion.

2. Have the group form triads and ask them to tell each other which consequences of abuse they identified with in this chapter. Were there other consequences not mentioned here?

3. Divide the group into pairs and ask them to share their answers from this chapter that were most significant to them. Also have them tell how they are doing with any new boundaries that they have begun to exercise and evaluate with one another any additional boundaries they have decided to set.

4. Bring the group back together for final questions, thoughts, and feelings that may need to be discussed before leaving.

Set time limits on these group sessions. Remind participants that they do not have to share anything they are not ready to share.

— 7 —

Mike's Story

$\mathcal{M}$y dad was what is called a periodic drunk. When he drank, he drank everyday. He would leave home and stay gone for months at a time because Mother wouldn't let him drink in the house. If she relented, he would leave anyway after he'd been drinking two or three days.

He was also addicted to gambling. He drank, gambled, and partied. He was a *FUN* kinda guy. Mom was not one to join in those *FUN* kinda of things.

When he decided to sober up, Mom and I would go get him, bring him home, and dry him out. He was able to stay sober anywhere from thirty days to three years.

These are the most difficult kinds of alcoholics to get sober because they can quit drinking and stay sober for periods of time on their own. Non-alcoholic persons don't need to quit drinking, because they don't need to prove that they can. The only person who ever quits drinking is an alcoholic. If an alcoholic knows that he can start drinking again, he can stop long enough to "prove" that he's not an alcoholic.

So Dad was gone a lot. Many of us have had parents who were gone a lot whether they were alcoholic or not. They either worked long hours on the job, worked two jobs, were working on some project, bowling, fishing, or lost in the football game on TV. They were just gone. Such absenteeism produces some of the same results in the family as the absentee alcoholic.

Even when my Dad was home, he wasn't there emotionally. He was planning his next drunk. He didn't know much about raising kids. He told me that after I was grown. "You know I never should have had a kid."

So, my dad was never my dad. When he was around, he tried to be my buddy. But I was so mad at him for being gone and drunk, I didn't want to be buddies. I wanted a dad. Dads who discipline their children stand for something in their children's eyes. It makes the kids feel secure. They may gripe about it and push the limits, but those things give them a sense of security. It also tells them that Dad cares what happens to them, that he has their best interests at heart.

Well, my dad never laid a hand on me. I came to realize when I was thirty, about two years into recovery from my own alcoholism, that some of my misbehavior was an attempt to get my dad to pay attention to me.

He was not emotionally available to Mom or me. This created a vacuum in both Mom and me for an intimate relationship with this person. We both had needs that only Dad could fill. She needed a husband and I needed a dad.

When a vacuum is created by the absence of one thing it sucks something else in to fill it up. People are not that different. This vacuum created in the two of us began to seek out something else with which to fill itself. Mom's void got filled up with me. She had a need for a husband, a partner, a mate, and emotional security. She turned to me for that. It became my job to meet her needs. I got the message that my needs didn't matter. As any classic codependent and adult child of an alcoholic knows, everybody else's needs are more important than their own.

Now nobody told me when I was four years old that my needs were not important and that my mother's needs and those of others were more important than mine. But, boy, did I get that message. So, I entered into a codependent relationship with my mom.

Her inappropriate dependence upon me is called cross-generational bonding and emotional incest.

When I was about fifteen, Dad called me into manhood by bringing a case of beer to my bedroom. Mom was out of town. He threw it in the door and told me I could invite a friend over, but "be sure to stay in the bedroom." He and some buddies were going to play poker for the next few days.

When it came time for my dad to tell me about sex, he came in and said, "Well, 'bout time we had a talk."

I said, "Yeah?"

"Well, you know what it's all about."

"Yeah?"

"Just don't get anybody pregnant. That's it."

That pretty much cleared it up for me.

The purpose for looking at our past is not so we can hate our parents and blame them for everything that's wrong with us now. We do this to make sense out of what is going on with us now. We do not have to repeat the past. Our brain is telling us that we only know one way to live. This is neuro-linguistic mapping (brain language). It's not *what* we think that needs changing, it's *how* we think about what we think that needs changing and what kind of action we take as a result of how we think. The recovery process takes this brain language and changes it.

Emotions are linked to how we think and our emotions have dictated most of our behavior. When we're dysfunctional people, our feelings are on top of our thinking and it needs to be the other way around. Our thinking needs to be on top of our feelings. If our feelings are constantly dictating our actions, we will have little or no boundaries, and we will be in some kind of self-destructive behavior. We are constantly violating our own boundaries and allowing others to violate them.

I did not know anything about boundaries or have a sense of self. I took on everything that went on in my family. When bad things happened, it seemed like it was always my fault. Dad drank because I was a defective unit. Dad left because I wasn't worth being around. No one told me that Dad's drinking was not about me. I became this false, shame-based person who existed to meet the needs of others. Instead of someone being there to mirror my feelings, my feelings were shamed and pushed further down inside of me.

This is part of my story. Many of you could tell your version of it and we would find that the violations are much the same. We will discover that the process of recovering from the wounds of these violations will involve looking at these violations.

We will be doing work in five areas where boundaries need to exist. These boundary areas are relational, spiritual, physical, sexual, and emotional. We will find in this process that boundary violations can be verbal, non-verbal, accidental and thoughtless, deliberate and malicious, or even an attempted act of kindness. We may have strong boundaries in some of these areas yet weak ones in others.

When we talk about one of these boundary areas, we will almost always cross over into the others as well. Any abuse sends us a message of "less than worthy" to our whole person as a system and violates us in all of these other boundary areas.

Nevertheless, by breaking boundaries and boundary violations down into these five areas, we can learn
- how to identify them,
- how to identify abuse, and
- how to establish healthy boundaries to avoid further abuse.

— 8 —

Relational Boundaries

$\mathcal{W}$e have divided our work on boundaries into five categories: relational, spiritual, physical, sexual, and emotional. We will begin with relational boundaries because they are so basic. Our lives are composed of systems of relationships, and boundaries define who we are in those relationships. Every boundary violation will affect our relationships with others.

RELATIONAL BOUNDARIES DEFINED

Relational boundaries determine who are safe people to let into our lives and the appropriate interaction and behavior we permit from them.

Moms and dads are supposed to be safe people to have in our lives as little children. My mom and dad were not safe, but I didn't know that. I didn't know that my mom and dad were any different from anyone else's mom and dad or that my house was any different from that of other kids. Then, I began to notice. "This guy's dad doesn't leave home and go gambling for six months at a time. They must be a weird family." I was unable to differentiate between appropriate and inappropriate behavior and who was safe and unsafe.

I went out into the world as a young adult and got into relationships with unsafe people. I gave them the keys to my house, the keys to my car, my charge card, my checkbook. I invited them over and they stole my stereo, wrecked my car, ran my up charge card, and broke my heart. "Gosh, these people are jerks. I thought these were nice people."

I allowed that because I didn't know the difference between who was safe and who was unsafe. These were the same kinds of people as those who had been treating me badly my entire life. I knew no better than to go out and find some more of them. Nice people looked like strangers to me.

RELATIONAL BOUNDARY VIOLATIONS DEFINED

A relational boundary violation occurs when the interaction between two parties is not appropriate to the relationship.

The relationship between my mom and me was not appropriate for a mother and her son. I received the subtle message early on that I was responsible for her needs. "I don't know what I'd do without you, Mike. You're the little man of the house. I'm so glad you're here—I'd die if you weren't here. You know, son, it's just you and me."

Those are the kinds of things a wife says to her husband, not to her child. That was a relational boundary violation. She was supposed to be there to meet my needs. I was not supposed to be there to meet her needs.

My mom met my needs in other important areas of my life. She was not a bad person; she was a great person. If you met her, you'd like her a lot. If you had any problems, she'd fix them for you while she was feeding you dinner.

If we come from dysfunctional families, we haven't learned how to have healthy relationships. We tend to bring harm to each other whether we mean to or not. The harm we bring can have serious consequences that pass on to our descendants. If we are to stop the abuses, we must learn how to set healthy boundaries.

Before we can set a healthy boundary, we have to know what boundaries are. We have to know when we have been violated and when we have violated another. We need to know what our boundaries are and understand that we shouldn't violate them again. This recognition and understanding needs to happen as soon after the violation as possible. The sooner the boundary violation is brought to our attention, the sooner we can learn what is appropriate and acceptable behavior and what is not.

A lot of healing can occur from a violation when the offender shows concern for the victim and goes immediately to ask forgiveness. The tenth step of Alcoholics Anonymous's Twelve Steps says that we "continued to take personal inventory and when we were wrong promptly admitted it."[1] This discipline helps keep us in a state of recovery and out of resentments.

We who are subject to abuse have a responsibility to say *no* to something that's inappropriate and unacceptable to us. We have the right to let the offender know when our boundaries have been violated.

Healthy boundaries not only help to identify who we are, but serve to protect the integrity of who we are. Without healthy boundaries, we would not know when we are being violated.

Relational boundary violations can be against God, ourselves, and others.

BOUNDARY VIOLATIONS AGAINST GOD

We violate God when we sin.

In the Judeo-Christian community, sin is a transgression of a religious or moral law, especially when it is deliberately committed. Theologically, sin is deliberate disobedience to the known will of God. It is something that is regarded as being shameful, deplorable, or utterly wrong.

These religious and moral laws are given in the Bible—a record of God's dealings with people. Some of us may have a negative view of why God gave these laws. We may have thought that God, sitting around bored one day, said to his angels, "You know, we've got these folks down there on the earth, and I just think we need to give 'em some hard things to do and not to do. We need to put a little pressure on 'em. So let's make up some stuff. What do you think?"

I no longer believe that God is some mean ol' ogre in the sky who doesn't want his created ones to have any fun in life. God's laws are in our best interests: "Look kids, here are ten commandments. Stay within these boundaries, and you will be all right. Violate these boundaries (sin), and you will hurt yourself, others, and me, too."

The Ten Commandments outline God's principles for safe and healthy boundaries in relationships. The first three address man's relationship with God. The fourth commandment directs individuals how to take care of themselves: work six days, rest on the seventh. The last six commandments have to do with getting it right in relationships with others: honor your father and your mother, don't kill each other, don't commit adultery, don't steal from each other, don't lie about each other, and don't covet each other's properties and mates.[2] The presupposition of these God-boundaries is that you will do well in life if you pay attention to these boundaries in relationships.

The Bible speaks of God forgiving sins, or boundary violations. King David speaks of his sin and God's forgiveness in the Psalms.[3] The New Testament disciples of Jesus were taught to ask God to forgive them of their debts as they were to forgive their debtors. Jesus followed up by saying, "If you forgive men their trespasses, your heavenly Father will also forgive you, but if you do not forgive men their trespasses, neither will your [heavenly] Father forgive your trespasses."[4]

Trespasses violate boundaries. Theoretically, we cannot trespass unless a boundary has been declared. God posted his boundaries. So, sin, in Judeo-Christian theology, is a boundary issue. When God's laws are violated, his boundaries are violated. God is seen as the author of boundaries. His boundaries determine the kind of relationship he wants his faithful ones to have with him, themselves, and others.

What were you taught as a child about God's laws?

What were you told would happen to you if you disobeyed God's laws?

How did that affect your view of God?

How do you view God now?

How might you strengthen your relationship with God?

We violate God by living self-serving lives.

The New Testament reports that Jesus summed up the Ten Commandments in either two or three commandments depending upon your interpretation: love God, self, and others. "You shall love the Lord your God with all your heart, and with all your soul, and with all your mind. This is the first commandment and great commandment. And the second is like it, you shall love your neighbor as yourself."[5]

Love is a relational term. The Greeks had more than one word for *love*, and the original Greek word used in the commandment is *agape*. *Agape* is not a feeling. It is a description of how we are to live in relationships with God, ourselves, and others. It is a love that puts no conditions or self-serving expectations upon the relationship. It is doing for others what is in their best interests without expecting anything in return. *Agape* contrasts with self-centeredness.

We cannot love others with *agape* until we have learned how to love ourselves with *agape*. To love ourselves with *agape* is not self-serving or narcissistic. The truth is we cannot give ourselves away to others if there isn't anything there to give. We must have a healthy relationship with ourselves, know who we really are, and take care of ourselves in a godly and healthy way before we can have healthy relationships with others.

How have you been affected by someone whose "love" seemed more self-serving than caring?

How have you used others for something for yourself in the name of love?

How can you be less self-serving?

How can you avoid being the victim of self-serving people?

We violate God when we violate others.

If we accept the premise that God is the author of boundaries, then all boundary violations are against him, either directly or indirectly. We violate him directly when we disobey his commandments, laws, and principles; and indirectly when we violate ourselves and others.

Bible imagery shows that God not only takes boundary violations of others as a personal offense, but that he desires to have intimacy in relationship with us, individually and collectively.[6]

How might you strengthen your relationship with God by the way you allow others to treat you?

How might you strengthen your relationship with God by how you treat others?

BOUNDARY VIOLATIONS AGAINST SELF

Here are some of the ways we violate boundaries against ourselves:

We violate and continue to weaken our own boundaries by not taking care of ourselves.

We don't eat as we should. We don't rest when we need to. We don't say *no* when we should. We isolate when we should be mixing. We don't exercise enough, or we exercise too much. We don't allow ourselves enough leisure time, or we allow ourselves too much leisure time.

How could you take better care of yourself?

We violate and continue to weaken our own boundaries by abusing our thought life.

We abuse ourselves by the things we listen to, read, and look at, as well as by the resentments we carry around inside our minds.

How could you take better care of yourself in your thought life?

We abuse ourselves by our addictive and obsessive/compulsive behaviors— the substances we use and things we do to medicate our pain.

Addictive substances and compulsive behaviors directly affect our physical, mental, and emotional health. Alcohol, drugs, sexual improprieties, overeating, and smoking are examples of things that are hazardous to our health. The more we use our drug of choice, the more we avoid the issues that cause the pain. The more we avoid the issues that cause the pain, the more we are compelled to use our drug of choice. Our addictive use and behaviors will kill us if not interrupted.

How are your addictions and obsessive/compulsive behaviors abusive to you?

What kinds of choices could you make about your addictions and obsessive/compulsive behaviors that would improve the quality of your life?

We can violate ourselves by what we say.

If we have been raised in a negative, non-nurturing environment, we will not have a healthy attitude toward ourselves, and we will speak negatively about ourselves. These negative words defile us and program us for failure.

When we talk too much or speak without screening our words, we often stick "our foot in our mouth" and create problems not only for someone else but for ourselves as well. "He who guards his mouth preserves his life."[7]

How are you abusing yourself with negative statements about yourself, or how are you putting yourself down?

How could you change what you think and say about yourself in order to improve your self-image and possibly the quality of your life?

We can violate ourselves by having unrealistic expectations of others.
When we have unrealistic expectations of others, we set ourselves up to be hurt. People will fail to live up to our expectations. When they fail, we feel disappointed and hurt by them. We must learn to take responsibility for the fact that, in most cases, we set ourselves up to be hurt. We have to learn what is an unrealistic expectation. The fewer expectations we can have upon others, the more pleasant we will make life for ourselves as well as for others.

Make a list of key persons in your life and the expectations that you have of them.

Which of the expectations are fair?   Put a check mark beside them.

Which of the expectations are realistic?   Put an "X" beside them.

Which of the expectations set yourself up to be disappointed and hurt? Underline them.

How can you change your expectations of these people, allowing them and yourself some slack?

We violate ourselves when we set ourselves up to be a victim.
We continue to harm ourselves when we keep on doing the same destructive things over and over again expecting different results.
We violate ourselves and our own boundaries when we go against our

nature, our values, our convictions, and life-changing decisions that we've made. A guy can make a decision around 8:00 A.M. to never drink again, "Boy, when I drink, I hurt myself; I hurt other people; I get D.U.I.s; I've had it." That's setting a boundary. About 3:00 P.M., he's deciding things weren't quite as bad as he thought they were. "I think I'll just have one beer when I get off from work." That compromise is a boundary violation.

Relationship addicts set themselves up to be victims. "I'm never getting in another abusive relationship. I'll never marry an alcoholic again. They are emotionally unavailable, physically abusive, and uncommitted." But if we don't get healed from the kinds of things that lead us into those abusive relationships, we will invite another abusive person into our lives.

What is something in your life that you keep repeating, hoping the next time that things will work out even though they never do?

How is that bringing harm to you?

Why do you keep doing it?

What can you do to stop it?

Other ways we violate our boundaries:
    This list of ways that we violate ourselves is not all inclusive. You may think of others.

How else might you violate your own boundaries?

What could you do to change these behaviors?

BOUNDARY VIOLATIONS AGAINST OTHERS

Here are some of the ways we violate the boundaries of others:

We violate others when we violate ourselves.
When we violate ourselves, it has a fall-out effect upon others simply because we are communal beings. We do not live unconnected to others. Even if that connectedness is dysfunctional, we are, nevertheless, connected. We are connected physically, spiritually, emotionally, environmentally, economically, politically, and socially. Every violation has some repercussions upon a larger body of people and circumstances.

In what way can you stop violating yourself in order to prevent violating others as well? (Consider addictions, sex, food, money, attitudes, time, etc.)

We violate others by what we do directly to them that we should not do and by what we fail to do that we should have done.
Our actions or failure to act can adversely affect others' feelings, time, property, bodies, relationships, and individual rights.

How can you change your behaviors in order to show respect for others?

We violate people by taking advantage of their goodness.
There are those who never say *no* and are always ready to lend a helping hand. There are those of us who take advantage of that.

How have you possibly violated someone by taking advantage of their goodness?

We violate the boundaries of others by our preoccupation with work, play, or watching TV—things that take away the time that belongs to others because of the nature of our relationship with them.

What things can you do or stop doing to build up your relationship with the significant others in your life (mate, children, etc.)?

We violate the boundaries of others by the things we say to others and the way we say them (such as ridicule, sarcasm, and put-downs).

An insensitive parent yells at the child, "You never do anything right!" Those "always" and "never" statements harm boundaries. These statements are recorded in little Johnny's mental and emotional "shame" library. The head shame librarian lives in there and possesses all of the shame tapes. When ridicule is made against little Johnny, she rushes in and plays all the old tapes.

Those shame messages were put there early in life. When the pressure is on, we will play out the old program that was put in during our developmental stage. We have to erase the old tapes and record affirming messages in their place.

When we beat up on somebody for their addictive behavior, we call up their shame librarian. Shaming people for their addictions does not help them. It often makes matters worse. Shaming is an enabling behavior. You cannot beat an alcoholic any harder than he has been beating himself. His shame has a lot to do with his drinking in the first place.

How can you change what you say about yourself and others that would build self-esteem?

We violate the boundaries of others by the things we say about them through gossip, slander, criticism, and judgmentalism.

We can violate boundaries by listening to conversations that are none of our business, or by not listening to someone to whom we should be listening, such as our mates and children.

What actions can you take in the future to stop gossip, slander, criticism, and judgmentalism?

We violate the boundaries of others by our attitudes of prejudice, bigotry, and separatism.

What decision can you make or action can you take to eliminate prejudice, bigotry, or separatism?

We violate the boundaries of others through abandonment and rejection.

All abandonment and rejection is abusive. Children experience abandonment in many ways. They experience abandonment when love is withheld from them by either or both of the parents, when a parent dies, when their parents divorce, when one of the parents is always absent, when their feelings are not properly mirrored, and when they are not physically nurtured or mentally stimulated. Both parents can still be in the house and abandon their children emotionally. For example, the security of the children can be threatened in a dysfunctional or alcoholic home if they are never sure the paycheck will make it home—when there are always money problems and the children are always hearing about them.

What healthy measures could you take to avoid future abandonment in your life?

What choices do you need to make to avoid abandoning others for whom you have a legitimate responsibility?

We violate the boundaries of others when we insist on unreasonable conformity to our self-centered agendas.

Dad's been in a boring meeting for four hours with his six-year-old son at his side. "Let's go, Dad. I wanna go." Dad sharply responds, "Be quiet and sit there or I'll beat the tar out of you." No provision is made for the child except to suffer.

How can you protect yourself from being the victim of someone else's self-centered agenda?

What changes can you make to avoid the victimization of others by your own self-serving agenda?

We violate the boundaries of others in our codependency.

Codependency has many facets to it. Basically, codependents are the type of persons who have lost their identity by taking care of the needs of other people. Codependents think they are helping others by doing for those others what they could and should be doing for themselves. They are, instead, enabling others to continue in their dysfunction.

In so doing, they have not only violated themselves by denying themselves of themselves, but have violated the other persons by not allowing them to suffer the consequences of their actions. Maybe Joe Bob needs to sleep out in the street and eat out of the dumpster just once to find out how his decisions are destroying him.

When we try to fix other people by enabling them, we are providing them with the kind of help they will need help from later on.

What tough love decisions do you need to make for the sake of another person?

We violate the boundaries of others through manipulation.

Manipulation is the result of feelings of insecurity and fear. We feel unsafe in our environment. We resort to manipulation to try to control our world. The irony is that manipulation sets us up for further rejection, insecurity, and fear. Manipulation is not a healthy way to be in relationship. It is a violation of another person's will.

Addicts (including codependents) are well known for their control issues. When we don't feel very good about ourselves, we tend to dominate others. We operate under the compulsion that there has to be a winner and a loser at all times. If we are losing, we perceive the relationship to be a bad one. We may shout, rage, hit, throw things—do whatever it takes to shut down the other person. This stifles the other person and brings harm to his or her boundaries.

What can you do to stand against manipulation from another person?

What changes can you make to avoid manipulating someone in your life—trying to get them to do what you think is right even though it appears to be going against their will?

We violate the boundaries of others through triangulation.
Triangulation occurs in a relationship when one person sends a message to another person through a third party, involving that third party in a situation that is clearly none of his or her business. This violates the boundaries of the third person.
"Go tell your Dad I said ..."
"Dad, Mom said ..."
"Well, you go tell your Mom I said, ..."
"Mom, Dad said ..."
That's triangulation.
Triangulation often occurs because a manipulator loses control of another person and wants to bring in a third party to get the other person to do what the manipulator wants.
The fiancée had a list of conditions worked out before she would consent to marrying her betrothed. She had been chasing him for a year and he had agreed to marry her, but he wasn't going for the conditions. Their marriage was less than a week away when she called his friend to tell him all of the ways that her fiancé had not lived up to her conditions and why he should. "What are you going to do about him?" she asked.
"Nothing. It's none of my business. Why did you call me and tell me all of this stuff?"
"Because you're his friend. You need to do something."
She wanted to pull the third party into the situation to do for her what she had not been able to do through her own means of manipulation. That's triangulation.

What changes do you need to make in how you relate to others in order to avoid involving them in triangulation?

How can you avoid being the third party victim in a situation that should not have been any of your business?

Other ways that we violate

This list of ways in which we violate others is not all inclusive. You may be able to add to the list out of your own experience.

AUTHORITIES, SUBORDINATES, AND PEERS

We relate to others on one of three levels: as authorities, peers, or subordinates. Everyone in your life falls into one of these categories. A relational boundary violation occurs when we overstep these lines and fail to relate appropriately according to the role we are in with others.

Authorities

Authorities have rank or power over others. Examples of authorities are parents, teachers, bosses, supervisors, judges, law enforcement officers, doctors, attorneys, and therapists.

We are supposed to be able to trust these people to know more than we do in their area of expertise and to appropriately take care of our needs in accordance with their office.

In order to get what we need from these authorities in our lives, we need to submit to their expertise and avoid trying to be their buddies. If we are the authority, we need to maintain a professional relationship with those who are subordinate to us. Authorities and subordinates cannot usually become peers without it affecting their relationship and boundaries.

The policeman can pull you over for driving too fast and give you a ticket for that. That's an appropriate action for him to take because you broke the law. It's inappropriate for that policeman to pull you over, even if you were speeding, and suggest that you give him a bribe or demand sexual favors from you in return for not writing you a ticket.

Parents, as authorities over their children, have the responsibility to discipline their children and nurture them to become healthy and responsible adults. They have the power to validate or invalidate the worth of their children. Parents violate their children when they fail to discipline and validate them.

The therapist is privileged to information about you that you desire for no one else to ever know. We need to feel safe telling him or her our darkest secrets without the fear of others hearing about them. We need to know that we will not be violated with inappropriate touching or talking. Those kinds of violations are far more damaging to an individual because of the therapist's position of authority. And in no way are we supposed to be there to meet our therapist's needs.

Ministers are supposed to be representatives of God—the ultimate authority. Any boundary violation from a person in that position sends spiritual, emotional, and sometimes physical shock waves through us. If we are unable to disassociate the person from God, our relationship with God will certainly be hindered or else we will develop a distorted view of God.

Other examples of relational boundary violations from authority figures are parents who batter their children, bosses who yell at their employees, bosses who try to be a father, therapists who try to have a personal peer relationship with their clients, and pastors who manipulate their congregations. What should be normal, nurturing relationships become twisted. The boss's job is to boss, the Dad's is to parent, the physician's is to treat, the husband's is to nurture his wife, and the policeman's is to enforce the law.

If we fail to get the help we need from these authorities, we end up being used and abused by them which leaves us emotionally bankrupt. Anne Katherine points out that nurturing relationships fill us while exploitative relationships take from us.[8] Exploitative relationships leave holes in us that we later try to fill with alcohol, drugs, work, food, sex, etc.

Moreover, when our trust has been violated by early authorities, we may have trouble trusting all other authorities later on, even God.

We need to keep the boundaries in these relationships clear.

Who are the significant authorities in your life?

Who are you an authority over?

How could you improve your boundaries in relationships with authorities in your life?

Subordinates

We create problems for ourselves and others when we fail to recognize our place as subordinates. The authorities in our lives need to maintain their integrity with us and we must maintain our integrity with them. We not only have the responsibility to protect ourselves from the abuses of authorities in our lives, but we must not abuse their authority. We may be subordinates, but we are not powerless to behave properly.

Children are supposed to be subordinate to their parents. They don't have the right to say or do anything they want. We live in an age when child abuse is at epidemic proportions. But there is also a thing called parental abuse and it is real abuse. Many parents are held hostage by the tempers and manipulations of their children. Codependent parents are likely candidates for parental abuse. It is not OK for children to talk back to their parents, to hit them, or to get their way with them as the result of their anger and manipulation. It is not OK for children to exercise control of any kind over their parents.

To allow children the right to say or do anything they want not only violates the parent's boundaries, but the children's as well. Parents are supposed to meet the children's needs by teaching them boundaries and discipline. If the children are allowed to rule the house, they will not learn about boundaries. Avoiding parental abuse is the parent's responsibility.

Who are the significant subordinates in your life?

How could you improve your boundaries in relationships with subordinates in your life?

Peers

A peer is someone on the same level or of the same status as we are, such as a friend, co-worker, or business partner. We are supposed to approach our peers differently from those in authority or those who are subordinate to us. Some people have trouble making that distinction. Some people try to be everybody's boss. Some people treat everybody like they are peers. Some people feel subordinate to everybody else.

We have certain privileges and limits that apply specifically to peer relationships. We may be able to hug our peers, joke with them, buy them gifts, ask them for favors, join them for dinner and a movie—hang out with them in ways that would be inappropriate with authorities and subordinates in our lives.

There are limits to what is appropriate among peers. Peers don't have a right to say or do anything that is cruel or hurtful to you. They cannot touch you in any way they want to. Your body is your body and you have a right to set healthy boundaries with everyone in your system of relationships.

Who are the significant peers in your life?

How could you improve your boundaries in relationships with peers in your life?

ROLES IN RELATIONSHIPS

Healthy boundaries have some flexibility and some limits depending upon the nature of the relationship. The roles we play in relationships define the limits of appropriate interaction with others. Husbands and wives have a different peer relationship with each other than the husband has with his golf partner. Coworkers have rules that apply on the job that are exclusive to the situation. Males relate to other males differently than females do to other female peers.

Our role with another person can change depending on the circumstances. We may be someone's boss on the job but a peer to him on a committee in our religious group. The role we play in relationships with others defines the boundaries that we set or accept.

We not only need to have healthy boundaries, but we also need to communicate to others what these boundaries are whether they know anything about boundaries or not. We don't have to buy Ronnie a teaching-tape series on boundaries for him to learn how to respect our boundaries. All we need to do is set our own boundaries and go on. We don't have to fix Ronnie. He can be mad, glad, or sad, and we can let him be that way. He can get over it or not get over it. Our boundary issues are about us, not about the other persons in our lives.

Write a brief summary of what you learned about yourself as a result of answering the questions in this chapter. What thoughts, feelings, and attitudes surfaced or became more clear to you?

Based on what you have learned in this chapter, summarize the new healthy boundaries you can begin to exercise in your relationships.

GROUP EXPERIENCE

Group Leader:

1. Ask if there are any questions about the information in this chapter. Allow others to answer through group discussion.

2. Ask someone in the group to give an example of a relational boundary violation. This could be one they experienced personally or witnessed. Have that person direct a reenactment of the incident, then ask:

What stood out to you as you watched the reenactment?

How might God have been violated in this incident?

How might self have been violated in this incident? (Self would be the person against whom the violation was committed).

Who are the others in this incident and how were they violated?

Use as many other examples as you allow time for.

3. Divide the group into pairs and ask them to share their answers from this chapter that were most significant to them. Also have them tell how they are doing with any new boundaries that they have begun to exercise, and evaluate with one another any additional boundaries they have decided to set.

4. Bring the group back together for final questions, thoughts, and feelings that may need to be discussed before leaving.

Set time limits on these group sessions. Remind them that they do not have to share anything they are not ready to share.

— 9 —

Spiritual Boundaries

---

*A*ll abuse has a spiritual effect upon us. Therefore we take on the subject of spiritual boundaries and spiritual boundary violations next.

SPIRITUAL BOUNDARIES DEFINED

Spiritual boundaries have to do with our ability to filter spiritual input. They have to do with discerning and determining what we let in and let out.

When we have healthy spiritual boundaries, we are in charge of what we believe and how we express what we believe. We understand that we alone are responsible for what we believe and what we do about it.

SPIRITUAL BOUNDARY VIOLATIONS DEFINED

Spiritual boundary violations occur when we are manipulated by deceptive teachings and controlling leaders to believe and behave in ways that would ordinarily be contrary to our wills and better judgments.

When we grow up in dysfunctional families, our filtering systems are polluted by what we were made to feel and think about ourselves that was not true. We were not given the life skills to discern for ourselves what is and is not the truth. This failure to discern truth causes us to live our lives in ways that are not consistent with the truth. A major component in our recovery from spiritual abuse involves the gradual process of learning how to discern the truth for ourselves.

Two levels of spiritual abuse are addressed in this chapter. We will first touch briefly on how all abuse has spiritual implications. Spiritual abuse is not confined to the realm of religion. Physical, verbal, emotional, and sexual abuse of children or adults has a spiritual impact upon them because abuse damages their human spirits.

Most of our attention, however, will be spent on the abuse that comes in the realm of religion. While spiritual abuse occurs in all sects, cults, and world religions, our examples are derived more directly from the traditional religious family systems in the United States.

As you continue reading, evaluate your own experiences to see what spiritual abuse you may have received from these systems.

THE SPIRITUAL IMPACT OF ALL ABUSE

Most of our relational, physical, sexual, and emotional abuse originated in childhood. As little children we were unable to do anything about it or to make any sense out of what was happening to us.

The perpetrator of the abuse was most likely an older person. It may have been a parent, other caretaker, older sibling, other relative, an authority, or an unknown intruder. The fact that these perpetrators were older and bigger persons meant that they represented a power that was greater than we were. They appeared to have power over life, therefore they were subconscious representatives of God to us. This, in turn, communicated a perverted view of God. Their misuse of power destroyed any positive impact these people could and should have had.

As victims of abuse, we developed a perverted view of authority and power altogether. Any relationship we might expect to have with God is hindered, perverted, or blocked entirely by this abuse. We may acquire a knowledge of God and have an awareness of God, but our experience is going to leave us with a distorted image of God.

The spiritual impact of abuse is far more damaging if that abuse came by way of a minister of religion who is a more direct representative of God to us.

All abuse affects the whole person: spirit, soul, and body. Healing for abuse must likewise be to the whole person: spirit, soul, and body. We cannot have complete healing from abuse until we deal with how we have been affected spiritually.

KINDS OF AUTHORITIES

We cannot be abused by another party unless that person is in some place of authority or power over us. The very nature of abuse implies an authority or power relationship of one person over another. Many agree that rape has more to do with power than with sex.

The authority or power may be positional, personally granted, imposed, or acquired.

Examples of positional authorities are parents, professionals, law enforcement officers, and teachers.

Granted authorities are those individuals or institutions we voluntarily choose to exercise power over us. The clergy is an example of this. Parents who allow an abusive child to rule them and their home is also an example of granted authority or power. We give power to angry people by our fear of what they will think of us or do to us.

Rapists, thieves, and other anonymous intruders are examples of imposed powers. In such cases, they are not authorities but overpower us with their physical strength, a weapon, or intimidation. A tyrannical ruler who takes power through force fits this category as well.

Acquired powers are those chemical addictions and compulsive-obsessive behaviors that take over our lives. We acquire them over a period of time as we habitually engage in them.

THE GOD FACTOR

The fact that abuse is at the hands of someone in authority or power over us causes the abuse to have spiritual ramifications.

"God, why did you allow that man to rob me in the parking lot? I'm one of your guys. You must not be who they say you are or be the way they say you are, or I must somehow deserve this punishment."

"Why did you allow my daddy to molest me all those years?"

"Why did you allow my spiritual leaders to lie to me and my family all of those years? Now I don't know who or what to believe."

I was two years old. I didn't know about Catholic, Baptist, God, or anything. I just knew about Daddy. Daddy was the first representation of God in my life. Nobody said that out loud to me, it just happened that way. But Daddy was alcoholic and unavailable to me. So I got the message that the most powerful, authority-bearing caregiver in my life was not available for me emotionally or physically. The only way I seemed to be able to get his attention was to act up.

Then Daddy, who was an Irish Catholic from New York, took me to church and parochial school. There was a particular set of nuns who were not that happy to be taking care of rotten little children like me. They were wearing these black and white outfits, and we were told never to touch the hem of their garments. We were told that it was as if they were married to Jesus. They became the God-figures in my life while I was at school. For whatever reason, I perceived them to be mean to me.

I was introduced to what they called the Holy Mother Church and that became a God-figure to me. I still did not have a personal relationship with Jesus or God. I didn't even hear about a personal relationship with God, but I heard about Holy Mother Church and I was given a lot of rules that I couldn't seem to obey or live up to.

The message that I heard was, "This is the authority in your life, you will obey what this says, you will do what this says, or you will go to hell. And if you don't do what we say and if you violate us too much, we'll throw you out—excommunicate you from the church. And we are the only church that gets to go to heaven, so if you get thrown out of this church, you will not go to heaven, you will go straight to hell."

This whole deal made me feel even worse about myself than I felt when I got there, and I wasn't feeling that good about myself the day I showed up. That was spiritual abuse which left me with a lot of religious baggage. I was abandoned and abused by the authority figures in my life. It got worse and more demanding as it went along.

Twenty-five years later, I sobered up. I went to a Twelve Step meeting and some guy told me, "You can get sober and you don't have to drink anymore."

"Oh, really? Wonderful. How do you do that?"

"Well, let go and let God."

"What? WHAT? GOD?"

"Well, you have to have a spiritual program or you'll never make it."

"What? Spiritual program? Wait a minute. I *had* a spiritual program. I know about your supposed God. He's the guy who abandoned me when I was a little boy and allowed my mom to emotionally incest me. He's the guy who let me stay drunk for 20 years. He's the guy who gave me this dad. He's the guy that's just like my dad—no, thank you."

"Well, you have to get the spiritual part of this program or you won't make it."

When I thought about God, no matter what I told myself, all this religious baggage came up with it. I had to pretend that the baggage wasn't there so I could begin to learn the difference between a spiritual program versus a religious program.

"How about a relationship with God?"

"I don't know about that. How does that work?"

Well, somebody had to teach me about it. I didn't know how to have relationships with people I could see, much less a relationship with someone I couldn't see.

I had to unload all this baggage about this God that I had picked up from these authority figures in the earlier years of my life.

It was as if I was on one side of a wall and God was on the other side. The only way I could get through to him was to go through this little hole in the wall. It was cut out just big enough for me to go through but not big enough to take anything with me. I couldn't have and maintain a relationship with God and have all of this baggage at the same time.

So, I could see God through this hole and hear him saying, "Come on. Trust me. Just step on through."

"I'm coming." I had one foot and an arm in, and I said, "Just a minute." I reached back through, "I've got to get this, and..."

He said, "No. No, you can't bring that in here. That won't go through the hole. If you want in here, you've got to leave that out there."

"Why? They told me that if I don't stand right, look right, believe right, if I ever say 'dammit,' I've had it; and I have a whole suitcase of that stuff. What am I going to do with it?"

He says, "I don't care about that. Put it down. Step on through. OK?"

"Well," I pondered the situation, "I...I...I'll come back tomorrow. I'll be back tomorrow. I've got to work on this stuff for a while. There's some stuff here that I'm not ready to leave behind."

When we do a portrayal of a dysfunctional family, we take pillows and stuff them under the arms of the father and the mother and pretend that they represent their baggage. The couple tries to get close to one another with all of that baggage coming between them but obviously cannot. That's how it is between God and us. He's there, but we can't get close to him until we get rid of the baggage. The Twelve Step process is an excellent exercise for getting rid of that baggage.

Religion tells us to work real hard to become something, and then we'll be OK with God and others. It tells us that we need to add things to our relationship with God—believe this, do that, get one of these, wear this, learn that, and glue this on your head. We keep doing those things until we look like all of the others, then we're in. We're initiated.

Those who have gone through Steps Four through Nine of the Twelve Steps find that it's not a question of adding stuff to us, it's a question of getting stuff off of us to become what God intended.

All we do is just let go and step through the hole, and we're automatically who we are in God. I don't have to *do* anything, other than say *no* to the lies and the baggage that I'm carrying and say *yes* to God's life and light. He will take over from there.

ABUSIVE RELIGIOUS SYSTEMS

We have already learned how our family-of-origin systems are dysfunctional to one degree or another. We adapted survival roles which are false selves. Unless we pay attention to correcting the things about the system we came out of, we will perpetuate those things in the other systems that we go into.

When our religious group is filled up with dysfunctional family-of-origin members, we end up with dysfunctional religious families. We continue to operate under all of the dysfunctional roles and rules of our families of origin. We are in as much denial in our religious communities as we are at home. We are not willing to admit that maybe something is broken here and needs to be fixed.

We should be able to meet with our religious groups and expect to have our spiritual needs met while there. In a healthy environment, the leaders are like fathers who exist to meet the needs of the spiritual children. The opposite is more often the case. The spiritual children exist in many institutions to meet the ego needs of the spiritual fathers. Instead of the fathers being needs-meeters, they have become the needy ones. Sometimes these spiritual fathers are more like enablers in dysfunctional family systems—they cause the children to relate to God as if God himself were the addict in the family.

It is not uncommon to find self-proclaimed spiritual authorities in religious groups today who are control addicts and get their egos fed from exercising power over people. We get involved in these religious family systems and it feels much like things were (are) at home. We experience the abuse and feel the all-too-familiar pain. We act out our father issues on the clergy. But we know how to survive in these abusive systems, so we stay there. We, in fact, are addicted to these systems as crazy-making as they might be.

Roles

We find, then, that our religious groups are families that are made up of addicts, enablers, heroes, scapegoats, lost children, and mascots—or combinations and variations of them just as they exist at home.

The following is a characterization of these dysfunctional family roles as they relate to religious family systems. Answer the question following each description as it relates to you and the religious group you are presently in or were in at any time in your life. You may want to answer for more than one experience.

The Addict. The addicts in religious family systems are the persons around whom everybody and everything else revolves. This person may be a needy clergyman (or clergywoman), a controlling deacon, or individuals who are in chronic crisis. In the small religious family system, the latter individuals can demand a lot of attention, time, and energy, draining resources while never allowing any problems to be resolved.

When the addict is a clergyman or someone in a position of power or authority, the members of the group are intimidated and caused to feel unfaithful, disloyal, or rebellious if they question his decisions. Everyone may know there's a problem but know it's not safe to talk about it.

Sometimes the addicts are those who rule surreptitiously. They wield power behind the scenes. Whatever happens in the system happens only if they grant a blessing upon it. The addict may be the clergyman's wife, an influential community leader, a member of the administrative board, or a major donor. Clergy who allow themselves to be compromised by these people are more codependent than addicted, although codependency is itself a form of addiction.

Some addicts may be sympathy seekers. "See how hard I work." They play on the emotions of others and create a support system by provoking guilt in altruistic people, often with no awareness of what they are doing.

Who is the addict in the religious group you were/are in?

The Enabler. The enablers are those who are "caretaking" the needs of the addicts. They always make them appear in a good light, excuse their failures, or shift the blame to other people or things. Their identities are wrapped up in the life of the addict.

If the addict is a clergyman, the enabler may be an assistant, the secretary, the administrative board chairman, the spouse, or all of the above. The enablers are the proverbial "yes men." It would not be unusual for the majority of the congregation to play that role. They insist that the addict can do no wrong. "There's not a problem here. If you think that there is a problem, you're the problem, not us."

Who were/are the enablers in your religious group?

The Hero. The heroes are the ones who show up to serve on every committee or board. They teach, sing in the choir, belong to all the clubs, and show up at every institutional workday. They try very hard to keep things together and working smoothly. They are high achievers who get favorable recognition from the leadership. They are the ones more likely to enter the ministry and other helping organizations.

Not everyone who serves is a hero in the dysfunctional family sense. Many people serve in accordance with God's gifting and calling. Heroes in the dysfunctional church family system are those who are playing out their survival roles as false selves. It may be difficult for most people to discern this difference. We can, nonetheless, tell true service from false service by the amount of attention that is focused on the one serving. True servants don't seek power, position, and recognition.

Who played/plays the role of the hero in your religious group?

The Scapegoat. These appear to be the troublemakers. They especially cause trouble for the establishment. You wish they would go away unless, of course, you're one of them, in which case you feel like running away. They are the proverbial "black sheep" in the family—an embarrassment to the family. They have no problem rocking the boat with truth and honesty. They carry a lot of the pain of the dysfunctional religious family.

Who played/plays the role of the scapegoats in your religious group?

The Lost Child. There's never any problems with these members! They are quiet, unassuming, possibly creative. They help make the institution look good. With a little courage they will sing in the choir—maybe create new music, help out in the Easter pageant, and make the posters for the women's bazaar.

Who played/plays the role of the lost child in your religious group?

The Mascot. The mascots provide the comic relief for an otherwise rigid and heavy atmosphere. As long as they don't joke about an issue that is too sensitive, they are tolerated. They might even be asked to be the master of ceremonies at the annual fund raiser.

Who played/plays the role of mascot in your religious group?

What role did/do you play in your religious group?
    Addict?
    Enabler?
    Hero?
    Scapegoat?
    Lost Child?
    Mascot?

What role did you play at home?

How are you the same (or different) at home and in your religious group?

We find that these roles are as dysfunctional in our religious family as they are at home. We are as false with our religious group as we are at home, maybe more so, and just as likely to violate one another's boundaries.

What changes could you make in how you related/relate to others in your religious group to avoid playing out your dysfunctional family-of-origin role?

Rules
As with the dysfunctional family of origin, these dysfunctional religious family systems have their own set of rules. These rules are usually unwritten

and unspoken. They are often experienced and enforced by fear, guilt and shame. There are different rules for different religious systems, but most of the characteristics of these rules are the same.

They are rigid and inflexible, as we see in legalistic faiths.

They change without notice.

Healthy rules do not exist where they are needed.

Some religious communities often have double standards. There are one set of rules for women while different rules or none exist for men.

The rules are essentially summarized into these three: don't talk, don't feel, don't trust.

The purpose of these rules is to maintain control.

Breaking the rules can carry serious shaming consequences.

One may not know a rule exists until it is broken.

What were/are some spoken or unspoken rules in your religious group?

Have you ever broken any of them?

Did it provoke fear, guilt, shame, or condemnation when you broke them?

How were/are you helped by these rules?

How were/are you harmed by these rules?

What boundary might you set to protect yourself from abusive spiritual rules?

ABUSIVE RELIGIOUS PRACTICES

The various practices of dysfunctional religious family systems are generally abusive. Spiritually abused victims, as with the victims of any abuse, are unable to discern these abuses. Nevertheless, abuse is abuse and all abuse has spiritual implications.

Spiritual victims

Everyone, including the clergy, are victims in these types of religious family systems and are in bondage to them. The leadership becomes very possessive of "their" sheep (constituents) and tries to maintain certain control over "their" flock. This control is primarily accomplished through membership in the organization which is presented as a way to solicit commitment but has the subtle effect of owning those who are joined to it.

Membership is obtained through various kinds of initiations. These initiations at minimum usually require adherence to the belief system and a pledge of allegiance and support to the system itself.

People are thought of as numbers and dollars. They are like trophies encased in egos. "How big is your church?" This often-asked question reveals much about motives. When ownership for the sake of vainglory is in operation, the sheep exist for the sake of the leadership rather than the leadership existing for the sake of the sheep. If someone behaves contrary to the rules, he or she might very well be disfellowshipped.

Leaders in these religious systems use their constituents to advance themselves in power, position, and riches, feeding their own egos. Instead of leading people to liberty, they keep them in bondage.

False headship

False headship is closely akin to ownership. False headship exists when the leadership of these religious family systems require their followers to submit unquestionably to their authority. In many of these cases, these leaders are self-imposed control addicts. They want authority without responsibility to their followers and submission without commitment to them; that is, they expect their followers to do and believe what they say without questioning them, but are unavailable to their constituents.

People who refuse to submit themselves to these self-appointed, elected, or hired authorities are criticized, shamed, shunned, and sometimes excommunicated.

Exclusivism

The leadership in these dysfunctional religious family systems control through fear, guilt, shame, and condemnation. One of the major deceptions put on the people is the exclusivity of that particular religious family. "We are the true ones. If you do not join us and believe as we believe, you are lost and going to hell. You are of the devil." If you really believe these things about your religious family system, then you are opening yourself up to all manner of abuse. If you do not perform "right," then you might become as one of the heathens. And "right" is always what the leaders say it is, even though they may seriously disagree among themselves.

If you are a spiritual hostage in one of these systems, you don't dare disagree with what you are being told to believe and how you are being told to behave. Disagreement is viewed as rebellion. The rules in these systems are too rigid and inflexible to permit personal inquiry. There is no room for growth beyond the confines of these religious walls.

Holiness codes

Many religious groups have very rigid codes for their constituents to live up to. These usually emerge over a period of time and become traditions. Anyone who is caught not living up to these peculiar codes is shamed. Therefore, one dare not allow his "sins" to be known. It is not OK to not be OK in these places. The people are forced to pretend that everything is just fine. They pretend holiness and learn to hide behind their phony religious facades.

These codes are legalistic. Spiritual legalism is performance oriented. We feel we must perform for God if we are to hope for his salvation. Our problem is that we can never quite get it right or ever do enough. This is deceiving and spiritually abusive because it requires us to perform the impossible. We are bound to fail in our performance, and, when we do fail, we are further shamed.

The clergy is caught in this web of expectations as much as anyone. The expectations put upon them by their own religious followers forces them to live behind their own facades. Once again, it is not OK to not be OK in these systems. Yet, many of these leaders are silently crying out in pain over things they dare not tell another. To do so would cost them their jobs and financial security. Many of them have confessed privately that if their congregations knew the truth about what they felt, thought, and did, they would be fired from their jobs. There is little room for grace, forgiveness, understanding, and acceptance for the truly repentant.

Manipulative appeals

Spiritual boundary violations often occur when appeals for money are made. We should be free to give according to our own conscience before God. We are spiritually violated when our emotions are manipulated into giving money or doing service beyond our desire or abilities to do so.

We are spiritually violated anytime our emotions are played upon to get us to do anything we don't want to do, or especially to pretend to be something we know deep inside we are not. Getting us to give, do, and be beyond our desires or abilities usually serves to meet the expectations and ego needs of the leadership in charge.

Enmeshment and abandonment

Congregations sometimes enmesh with their leaders and become an extension of them. "I am you." Enmeshment, as with all forms of abuse, is abandonment. We should be able to retain our individuality while finding acceptance and support in religious communities, yet we often experience abandonment there.

Institutionalism

Institutionalism is, by its very nature, abusive. Institutions tend to become bigger and more powerful than the people who make them up. They eventually exist for their own sakes. People are asked to join themselves to these institutions, give great sums of money to them, and work fervently for them, thinking they are doing these things for God. Constituents are led to believe that a relationship with these institutions is being in relationship with God. These institutions, however, have become the gods these people worship. People make icons of their religious buildings, doctrines, programs, and traditions. This is abusive because idolatry robs people of a real relationship with God.

Other abusive practices

The above examples are only a small sampling of the kinds of abuses people suffer from religion.

What other abusive religious practices have you experienced?

Based on the descriptions in this chapter and *your* personal experience, assess abusive religious practices in your religious group. (Others may be in your group, but experience things differently.) This is not for judgment, but is an evaluation so you can begin to set healthy boundaries for avoiding further abuse. Circle the number that is most appropriate.

	non-existent	slightly existent	definitely existent	over the line
Spiritual victimization	1	2	3	4
False headship	1	2	3	4
Exclusivism	1	2	3	4
Holiness codes	1	2	3	4
Manipulative appeals	1	2	3	4

Enmeshment/abandonment	1	2	3	4
Institutionalism	1	2	3	4

Write a brief summary of what you learned about yourself as you answered these questions. What thoughts, feelings, and attitudes surfaced or became more clear to you?

Based on what you have learned in this chapter, summarize the new healthy boundaries you can begin to exercise in your relationships.

GROUP EXPERIENCE

Group Leader:

1. Ask if there are any questions about the information in this chapter. Allow others to answer through group discussion.

2. Read the following true story aloud and ask group members to listen for boundary violations.

> *Maria lived in Brazil and was a member of a Pentecostal church. She was 39 years of age, an unemployed maid, and the mother of seven children. Three of the children had pneumonia and one of them had a heart ailment. The family survived on handouts. She won a $60,000 lottery ticket. Her preacher told her to burn the ticket or she would go to hell for taking the "devil's money." The congregation chanted, "Burn, burn, burn." In her confusion, she burned the ticket. When her husband found out what she had done, he beat her and left home.*

Discuss the story using the following questions to get started.
Who were the people who violated a boundary in this story?
What boundary do you think they violated?
Why do you think it was a boundary violation?

3. Divide the group into pairs and ask them to share their answers from this chapter that were most significant to them. Also have them tell how they are doing with any new boundaries that they have begun to exercise and evaluate with one another any additional boundaries they have decided to set.

4. Bring the group back together to discuss final questions, thoughts, and feelings.

Set time limits on these group sessions. Remind them that they do not have to share anything they are not ready to share.

— 10 —

Physical Boundaries

$\mathcal{W}$omen and children are the typical victims of physical abuse. Battered women are usually the victims of an abusive husband or significant male companion. Battered children are usually the victims of a violent parent or caretaker. The perpetrators of abuse are often abuse survivors themselves whose extreme reactions are the result of stress in their lives.

Physical abuse is not found only among the disadvantaged, uneducated, abnormal, psychotic, or criminal element. Internal stresses that erupt into violent actions are just as great among the "well to do." Cases of abuses of all kinds are coming out of the closet and perpetrators themselves are seeking help much more quickly as more information is made public.

For our purposes, physical boundaries involve two dimensions—our physical bodies and the invisible, psychological space around us.

PHYSICAL BODY SPACE

Physical boundaries, first of all, have to do with our physical bodies. The skin on our bodies is an obvious boundary that defines where we end and everything "out there" begins.

Physical boundaries are the first boundaries that we became aware of as infants although we did not consciously think about them as boundaries. Physical touching is the first way we learned who we were, who we belonged to, and what we were all about. "This is my mom, this is my dad. I am a different person than they, yet I belong to them and they belong to me."

Bodily abuse

There is a wide spectrum of bodily physical abuse. It includes sex crimes, murders, muggings, kidnappings, infanticides, conjugal violence, and assault and battery.

It is any non-accidental physical injury, including one that results in bruises, welts, broken bones, scars, burns, poisoning, internal injuries, or an injury that would normally require medical care.

It includes any neglect which results in physical deprivation. Parents who neglect the health and nutritional needs of their children are being physically and emotionally abusive to them. Children need for their caretakers to do for them what they cannot do for themselves. They have basic needs for food, shelter, clothing, attention to medical care and personal hygiene, love and coddling, mental stimulation, emotional nurture, guidance, stability, and discipline to teach them safe and appropriate boundaries. These things are absolutely necessary for survival. Studies show that children who have been without acceptance and emotional security have died for no other known reason. Children fail to thrive when their nutritional needs are neglected. They stop gaining weight and stop growing in stature and in head circumference. These children are likely to experience neglect in hygiene as well, making them more susceptible to disease and illnesses.

Physical abuse includes sexual violations against the body. Sexual abuse can cause physical, emotional, and sexual problems for an entire lifetime.

Physical abuse may even result from verbal abuse to children because it damages them emotionally, and the emotions can produce a chemical imbalance that produces physical illnesses.

We physically abuse ourselves by the way we eat or don't eat, by addictive substances we use, lack of sleep, lack of exercise, excessive use of exercise, and by caretaking.

INVISIBLE, PSYCHOLOGICAL SPACE

Physical boundaries have also to do with that invisible, personal, psychological space around our bodies. It is like an extension of us. This psychological boundary is very real and further defines our separateness from other persons, animals, and things. "This is my territory. You don't have a right in here unless I give it to you."

The psychological boundary for Ken, who is a good friend, might be pretty close. Ken comes into my psychological space with his invisible area to greet me, maybe even hug me or tease me. He can get right up in my face and it might be OK with me. But if Ken is someone I am meeting for the first time, there is an invisible comfort zone around me that doesn't want Ken up in my face. "Who are you? Get back." I also have a different physical boundary for my wife than I have for my friends.

These invisible, psychological boundaries develop at the same time that we, as children, are learning physical boundaries. In a healthy environment, each member of the family is aware of the physical self and the personal, invisible space that is uniquely his or hers. There is a distinction between "yours" and "mine" that extends to all areas of privacy and possessions.

This psychological space can be violated by the father who walks into the bathroom on his maturing daughter, parents who parade nude in front of their children, or general disrespect for one another's possessions.

If we were violated this way as children, we won't have a clear distinction between what is and what is not appropriate psychological space. We continue to allow others to invade that space because we live from fear and don't want to make anybody angry. We can't stand conflict. We are people pleasers.

PHYSICAL BOUNDARIES DEFINED

Physical boundaries have to do with choosing who can touch us, how we can be touched, and where we can be touched.[1] *They communicate how close others can get to us and what they can do to us.*

Our bodies belong to us, and we are the only ones who should determine how they are to be treated. We will increase our ability to determine who can touch us, how they can touch us, and how close they can come to us as we learn to set physical boundaries. Strong physical boundaries strengthen our character as a whole and our ability to have boundaries in other areas as well.

PHYSICAL BOUNDARY VIOLATIONS DEFINED

Physical boundary violations occur when we or our psychological space around us is touched by another person in such a way as to bring bodily or psychological harm to us.

People who grow up in dysfunctional families generally don't know what is and what is not appropriate when it comes to how other people treat them physically. As adult children of abuse, we come to believe that our natural instincts, feelings, and bodies don't count—that our bodies are to be used for other people's benefit or pleasure. Someone may be touching us inappropriately and we stand there angry, shamed, and violated. Instead of telling the person to stop doing that, we're telling those feelings to be quiet. "Shut up, feelings. If I don't let him do that, I won't get a paycheck next week." We get the message that other things are more important than our bodies and what is right and appropriate for our needs.

CHARACTERISTICS OF THE ABUSED CHILD

If we are adult survivors of abuse, we should be able to identify with the following description of abused children.

Abused children have a very difficult time expressing feelings. They don't know how to say what they like or don't like. They don't know how to recognize and verbalize loneliness, fear, anxiety, or pleasure. They don't know how to have fun, play, and laugh. They usually think they are bad, unlovable, and stupid. They are confused and their behavior reflects their confusion. They expect a lot from others yet have difficulty managing themselves. Their abuse has taught them to set themselves up for punishment which reinforces their poor self-image. They become fault-finders and want to exact severe punishment upon other children.

In what ways do you identify with these characteristics of the abused child?

Were you a physically abused child?

Who abused you?

Are you being physically abused in your life now?

What measures might you begin taking to protect yourself against physical abuse?

Who are the people in your life that violate your psychological boundaries?

What measures can you take to set healthy psychological boundaries?

Whose psychological space have you been guilty of violating and how have you done so?

What will you do to prevent invading the psychological space of another in the future?

ARE YOU AN ABUSIVE PERSON?

If we are adult survivors of abuse, there is a great likelihood that we have a tendency toward abusiveness ourselves. We may not know that the things we say and do are abusive since these were normal experiences in our dysfunctional family of origin. The following questions should help you to determine if you are a potential abuser. As with so many of these questions, you will have to work at being honest with yourself.

Do you often feel bad about yourself and put yourself down?

Are you rigid in your expectations of others, especially members of your family?

Do you find yourself needing to ask forgiveness a lot (whether you do so or not) for your violent behavior?

Do you have violent outbursts of temper?

Do you call other people ugly and hurtful names?

Do you see others, especially family members, as difficult to handle?

Have you hit and hurt others in the past—child, mate, parent, friend?

Are you being physically abusive to others now—child, mate, parent, friend?

If you answered *yes* to more than three of these questions, you are an abusive person. If you are honest and find that you are a rager with a potential for abuse, you will want to act responsibly by seeking professional help before anyone gets hurt, or hurt again.

What will you do to prevent physical abuse of another in the future?

Write a brief summary of what you learned about yourself as you answered these questions. What thoughts, feelings, and attitudes surfaced or became more clear to you?

Based on what you have learned in this chapter, summarize the new healthy boundaries you can begin to exercise in your relationships

GROUP EXPERIENCE

Group Leader:

1. Ask if there are any questions about the information in this chapter. Allow others to answer through group discussion.

2. Have different persons experiment with coming close to each other to determine how close the other person can come before they begin to feel uncomfortable.

Ask processing questions such as:

Which can come in closer, a member of your own sex or a member of the opposite sex?

Does age, physical size, race, physical appearance, etc., have anything to do with how close someone can come to you?

What other factors apply?

3. Divide the group into pairs and ask them to share their answers from this chapter that were most significant to them. Also have them tell how they are doing with any new boundaries that they have begun to exercise, and evaluate with one another any additional boundaries they have decided to set.

4. Bring the group back together to process final questions, thoughts, and feelings that may need to be discussed before leaving.

Set time limits on these group sessions. Remind them that they do not have to share anything they are not ready to share.

– 11 –

Sexual Boundaries

As damaging as physical abuse can be, sexual abuse can be more so. And, as with physical abuse, children are a main target of sexual abuse.

Ruth and Henry Kempe, authors of *Child Abuse*, define sexual abuse "as the involvement of dependent, developmentally immature children and adolescents in sexual activities that they do not fully comprehend, to which they are unable to give informed consent, or that violate the social taboos of family roles."[1]

Sexual abuse of children includes pedophilia, rape, child pornography, and all forms of incest. These children are exploited because sexual abuse robs them of their chance to develop control over their own bodies. They are also robbed of the chance to choose later in life with whom they will experience their first sexually intimate relationship.

The Kempes report that boys handle sexual abuse with greater difficulty than girls. Incest leaves "boys with such severe emotional insult as to block normal emotional growth. They tend to be severely restricted and may be unable to handle any stress without becoming frankly psychotic."[2]

Statistics show that approximately one out of every three females and one out of every eight men will experience some form of sexual abuse before reaching adulthood.

While I was the administrator of a treatment center, I initiated a group for sexual abuse survivors and contracted with a female therapist to lead it. The announcement invited anybody to come who wanted to work on sexual abuse survivor issues, but it failed to mention that it would be a women's group. When the time came, there were two women and *thirteen* men. I quickly had to organize a second group for men.

Most males who have been sexually violated were violated by another male, and usually while in their early adolescence.

Men, especially, who were sexually violated end up in non-responsive isolation. Their boundaries are so rigid that they won't allow anyone into their lives. They may marry and may even have children, but it will be impossible for them to achieve intimacy until they resolve these issues.

As it is with physical boundary violations, so it is with sexual boundary violations: our bodies belong to us and we should be the only ones who determine how we are to be treated by others. Sexual violations are also physical violations as well. They have severe, long-lasting, and widespread consequences that may impair total boundary development.

The more severe the violation, the more severe the boundary problems are going to be.

SEXUAL BOUNDARIES DEFINED

Sexual boundaries are limits on what is safe and appropriate sexual behavior as well as comments that are made both to us and by us.

SEXUAL BOUNDARY VIOLATIONS DEFINED

Sexual boundary violations are defined as any exploitation of a person for sexual gratification. It is being physically inappropriate for the relationship.

If we were sexually abused as children, we are not likely to know who we are sexually. We grew up believing that our body does not belong to us, that we do not have a right to say what others can do to us. Our bodies were treated like objects. Steven Farmer in his book *Adult Children of Abusive Parents* writes, "You could not feel safe being touched and caressed. Touching meant sex rather than affection. You had nowhere to turn with your simple needs for being held and cuddled. You were robbed of your innocence, robbed of the right to discover your sexuality gradually, to become sexual at a time when you were psychologically and emotionally capable of assimilating the experience."[3] Consequently, we grow up using sex to get affection.

Part of recovery for those of us who have been sexually abused is to come to the realization that no one owns our body even though we may have been imprinted with that message. This goes beyond sex. There are people who inappropriately approach us in play—grabbing, hitting, shoving, getting in our face, and inappropriately touching and handling us. Nobody has a right to do that and we have a perfect right to tell them, "Don't do that. It bothers me. I don't want that. I don't do that. I don't like that."

KINDS OF SEXUAL VIOLATIONS

Rape

Rape, as a sexual boundary violation, happens when someone forces themselves upon another for sexual gratification or forces another person to submit to sex acts, especially sexual intercourse.

Rape among adults can occur between a husband and his wife, a date and his girl friend, or a stranger/intruder—whenever it is not a matter of mutual consent. The rape of children occurs when an older child or adult performs sex acts upon the child or requires the performance of sex acts from them. These include actual intercourse, oral sex, anal sex, or fondling.

How have you experienced rape in your life?

How have you been the perpetrator of rape?

Incest

A dictionary definition of incest is "sexual intercourse between two persons too closely related to be married." E. Sue Blume, in her book *Secret Survivors: Uncovering Incest and Its Aftereffects in Women,* says, "Incest can be seen as the imposition of sexually inappropriate acts, or acts with sexual overtones, by—or any use of a minor child to meet the sexual or sexual/emotional needs of—one or more persons who derive authority through ongoing emotional bonding with that child." She further explains, "Incest can occur through words, sounds, or even exposure of the child to sights or acts that are sexual but do not involve her [bodily]. If she is forced to see what she does not want to see, for instance, by an exhibitionist, that is abuse."[4] Though Blume speaks of a female, her statements also apply to boys.

Girls are the more likely victims of incest, usually with the father or male guardian, an uncle, a brother, grandfather, or male cousin. The sexual acts begin with inappropriate hugging and kissing, graduate to fondling in the early years, then on to intercourse in adolescence. The child is usually lured into the act with threats, deceptive statements, or promised favors. The child may feel pleased at the time that he or she is getting that kind of special attention and affection, but the emotional damage later on is severe. Typical emotions are revulsion, anger, feeling defiled, and self-blame.

Incest is the most damaging form of child sexual abuse because it violates the bond of trust between the child and the child's perpetrator-guardian. The very one(s) who should be taking care of the child's needs are taking advantage of their power over the child.

Incest can also be in more subtle forms than overt sex. A mother, for example, borders on sexual incest by insisting on her little son sleeping with her far beyond the appropriate age for him to be doing so, especially when she is doing it to meet her own emotional needs.

How have you experienced incest in your life?

How have you been the perpetrator of incest?

Inappropriate touching

Inappropriate touching is a sexual boundary violation that can occur between adults of the opposite sex or the same sex, or can originate with adults toward children or with older children toward younger children.

Anyone, including a parent or a baby-sitter, sexually abuses an infant or toddler by inappropriately fondling his or her genitals. It puts a mark on that child for life, depending on how overt the violations are. That little child's body and psychological self knows and remembers that.

Inappropriate touching includes touching the other person's sexual parts, touching any part of the body with sensual intent, or hugging and kissing with sensual intent when it involves a person who is not of age to give consent or a person who is of age but does not give consent.

How have you been the victim of inappropriate touching?

How have you been the perpetrator of inappropriate touching of others?

Inappropriate dress

Sexual boundary violations have to do with inappropriate dress; for example, an exhibitionist who exposes himself, a woman who wears seductive clothing, a parent who undresses in front of a child.

The client had been in therapy for sexual addiction for a number of months. He and the therapist had been unable to relate his addiction to any childhood traumas. He insisted, "I don't think I'm in denial. Nobody ever did anything to me unless I've just totally blocked the whole thing out."

His addiction manifested itself in pornography and self-sex (masturbation). He was preoccupied with looking at naked women.

One day he was casually talking about his home life and happened to mention, "Of course, Mom was naked, because Mom was always naked..."

The therapist asked in astonishment, "What? You said Mom was naked?"

"Oh, yeah. My mother didn't wear any clothes until I was about sixteen or seventeen years old."

"When did she not wear any clothes?"

"At home. She's just ran around the house naked. I just remember Mom being naked, ever since I can remember. Why are you so interested?"

"Well, I think we may have found something here."

That was sexual abuse.

How have you been the victim of inappropriate dress?

How have you been inappropriate in your dress around others?

Verbal

Sexual boundary violations can be verbal. These violations can be things that are said between a parent and a child, between a dad and a daughter, or in the form of inappropriate conversation in the workplace. The male boss sends a subtle message to his female secretary that her job may be on the line if she doesn't provide him with sexual favors. Or, it is made clear that the career ladder is made up of rungs that lead to the bedroom.

How have your sexual boundaries been violated by someone's inappropriate comments to you or about someone else?

How have you violated the sexual boundaries of another by the inappropriate comments you have made?

Voyeurism and pornography

Sexual boundary violations can be visual, as is true of pornography and voyeurism.

Pornography involves looking at sexually explicit still or motion pictures or reading writings about sexually explicit materials for sexual gratification. Though some believe that pornography is primarily a violation against self, studies show that the use of pornography lessens one's desire for his or her mate and leads to sexual boundary violations against others.

United States Postal Inspectors have found that 80% of the child pornography collectors they investigate abuse children sexually. Dr. Victor Cline, University of Utah psychologist, has found that four things happen to males who become immersed in pornography: First, they become addicted. Second, their need escalates—wanting rougher, more bizarre, more explicit imagery. Third, they become desensitized. "What was first shocking, awful...becomes commonplace," he explains. Finally, they act out, doing the things they have seen. "Conscience has been immobilized....What was once shocking and wrong or immoral is now legitimized."[5]

Pornography is also used by perpetrators to desensitize and/or stimulate potential victims, including children. In these cases, a lesser boundary violation is used to gradually pave the way for a greater boundary violation against another person.

A voyeur is a person who derives sexual gratification from observing the naked bodies or sexual acts of others, especially from a secret vantage point. A peeping Tom fits into this category. Voyeurism is a direct invasion of privacy and is a sexual boundary violation. Viewing pornography is a form of voyeurism.

How have you been knowingly sexually violated by voyeurism or pornography?

How have you violated others with the use of voyeurism or pornography?

AFTEREFFECTS

The long range consequence of being sexually abused is that it robs us of our sense of self. We do not know who we are. We believe that we are not allowed to set limits with other people. We may suffer periodic depression. We avoid our feelings. We have trust issues. We have intimacy issues. We have relationship problems. We have a low sense of self-worth. We have a sense of helplessness. We acquire addictions and other compulsive behaviors. If we have suffered extreme sexual violations, we may suffer from amnesia. We may not have conscious memory of abuse, but the body still remembers it.

Alicia's best friend in high school had a slumber party one weekend while her parents were away. Alicia knew that boyfriends would be sneaked in and that most of the girls would have sex with them. She had been dating a boy and expected that he would be asked to come. But the thoughts of having to face the issue of sex was so terrifying that she physically trembled and vomited. She had no idea why she was reacting this way. She knew in her mind that she could simply say *no*, but her body was remembering something extremely shaming and scary that her mind had put away. Years later she was in therapy and unveiled the awful memory that she had been sexually molested by her older brother from the time she was three years old.

Martha was a woman in her thirties who had been having multiple affairs with men. She was attracted to abusive men but didn't know why. After having sex with a man, she would curl up into the fetal position and cry, "Please don't hurt me." There was a known pattern of sexual abuse in her family of origin among the uncles, but she had no cognitive memory of personal abuse. Nevertheless, her body and emotions were remembering something very real.

ARE YOU A SEXAHOLIC?

If we were victims of sexual boundary violations, we are going to have sexual issues. It is not uncommon for sexual abuse survivors to become sexaholics themselves.

Sexaholics Anonymous describes the problem this way:

> Many of us felt inadequate, unworthy, alone, and afraid. Our insides never matched what we saw on the outsides of others. Early on, we came to feel disconnected—from parents, from peers, from ourselves. We tuned out with fantasy and masturbation. We plugged in by drinking in the pictures, the images, and pursuing the objects of our fantasies. We lusted and wanted to be lusted after.
>
> We became true addicts: sex with self, promiscuity, adultery, dependency relationships, and more fantasy. We got it through the eyes; we bought it, we sold it, we traded it, we gave it away. We were addicted to the intrigue, the tease, the forbidden. The only way we knew to be free of it was to do it. "Please connect with me and make me whole!" we cried with outstretched arms. Lusting after the Big Fix, we gave away our power to others.
>
> This produced guilt, self-hatred, remorse, emptiness, and pain, and we were driven ever inward, away from reality, away from love, lost inside ourselves.
>
> Our habit made true intimacy impossible. We could never know real union with another because we were addicted to the *un*real. We went for the "chemistry," the connection that had the magic, *because* it by-passed intimacy and true union. Fantasy corrupted the real; lust killed love.
>
> First addicts, then love cripples, we took from others to fill up what was lacking in ourselves. Conning ourselves time and again that the next one would save us, we were really losing our lives.[6]

Test yourself by answering these twenty questions of Sexaholics Anonymous:[7]

TWENTY QUESTIONS

____ 1. Have you ever thought you needed help for your sexual thinking or behavior?

____ 2. That you'd be better off if you didn't keep "giving in"?

____ 3. That sex or stimuli are controlling you?

____ 4. Have you ever tried to stop or limit doing what you felt was wrong in your sexual behavior?

____ 5   Do you resort to sex to escape, relieve anxiety, or because you can't cope?

____ 6. Do you feel guilt, remorse or depression afterward?

____ 7. Has your pursuit of sex become more compulsive?

____ 8. Does it interfere with relations with your spouse?

____ 9. Do you have to resort to images or memories during sex?

____ 10. Does an irresistible impulse arise when the other party makes the overtures or sex is offered?

____ 11. Do you keep going from one "relationship" or lover to another?

____ 12. Do you feel the "right relationship" would help you stop lusting, masturbating, or being so promiscuous?

____ 13. Do you have a destructive need—a desperate sexual or emotional need for someone?

____ 14. Does pursuit of sex make you careless for yourself or the welfare of your family or others?

____ 15. Has your effectiveness or concentration decreased as sex has become more compulsive?

____ 16. Do you lose time from work for it?

____ 17. Do you turn to a lower environment when pursuing sex?

___ 18. Do you want to get away from the sex partner as soon as possible after the act?

___ 19. Although your spouse is sexually compatible, do you still masturbate or have sex with others?

___ 20. Have you ever been arrested for a sex-related offense?

If you answered *yes* to three or more of these questions, you are likely addicted to sex and in need of advanced care. Act responsibly to get help before you hurt yourself or someone else gets hurt by your obsessive behaviors.

Write a brief summary of what you learned about yourself as you answered these questions. What thoughts, feelings, and attitudes surfaced or became more clear to you?

Based on what you have learned in this chapter, what new healthy boundaries can you begin to exercise in your relationships?

GROUP EXPERIENCE

Group Leader:

1. Ask if there are any questions about the information in this chapter. Allow others to answer through group discussion.

2. Ask members in the group to suggest behaviors that they think are sexual boundary violations. Ask for some of the more subtle examples such as the boss who hugs his employees—male, female, or both; men giving the wolf whistle to women. List these on a board prior to discussion.

Take a vote on each item to see how many agree that it is a sexual boundary violation and how many disagree.

Ask the person who listed the offense to tell why he or she thought it was. Ask others to explain why they agreed or disagreed.

Evaluate each offense listed to determine when a behavior crosses over the boundary into an offense.

3. Divide the group into pairs and ask them to share their answers from this chapter that were most significant to them. Also have them tell how they are doing with any new boundaries that they have begun to exercise, and evaluate with one another any additional boundaries they have decided to set.

4. Bring the group back together for final questions, thoughts, and feelings that may need to be discussed before leaving.

Set time limits on these group sessions. Remind them that they do not have to share anything they are not ready to share.

— 12 —

Emotional Boundaries

Any kind of boundary violation has an emotional effect upon us. It may be physical, sexual, or verbal abuse. It may be abandonment or neglect. It may be spiritual or relational abuse. Because our emotions are affected in every instance, we discuss emotional boundaries last, though they are far from insignificant. For example, the body may heal from physical abuse, but the emotional wounds grow deeper and more severe if they are not dealt with. The emotional wounds are why we go to therapy, get into recovery, work the Twelve Steps, or work on boundary issues.

EMOTIONAL BOUNDARIES DEFINED

Emotional boundaries set limits on what is safe and appropriate for us to feel. They limit what things we let in and let out that provoke feelings. They determine how we let people treat us, including the range of personal comments that we will accept from others.

EMOTIONAL BOUNDARY VIOLATIONS DEFINED

Emotional boundary violations occur when someone intrudes or distances himself or herself from an individual with emotions or lack thereof that are inappropriate to the relationship.

EMOTIONAL HEALTH AND BOUNDARIES

Our emotional health is directly related to our boundaries. The healthier and more defined our boundaries are, the healthier and more defined we are as individuals, and the healthier our relationships will be. Anne Katherine writes, "The development of emotional boundaries and the development of self go hand in hand. Weak boundaries equal a weak self-image; a healthy self-image equals healthy boundaries."[1] Codependents, addicts, alcoholics, people with eating disorders, and others with life-controlling problems typically do not have healthy emotional boundaries.

We may have been so deeply scarred in past relationships that we will not risk getting emotionally involved with anyone—ever again. Or we may be so emotionally promiscuous that we dump our feelings on everyone, seeking our significance in others by becoming emotionally dependent on them.

STRONG EMOTIONAL BOUNDARIES

Proper mirroring of our feelings in childhood gave us a sense of self. We learned that our feelings were OK. We learned who we really were, and we are able to live in the strength of that.

My son John Patrick had a girlfriend when he was 15 years old. He was crazy about this girl but she couldn't quite get around to him. She would string him along. He'd call her now and then and she finally got around to "it's your turn, Johnny." Man, he was excited.

"Johnny," I told him, "she seems fickle."

"No, those other guys were nothing, Dad."

It lasted about thirty days. She dropped him to take up with his best friend. He was crushed but he got over it. Sometime later, she called him up and had a change of heart. "The others are jerks," she told him, "I'm ready to go back with you."

He said, "Excuse me for a minute," then asked me, "Dad, where's that music tape by Lee Roy Parnell?"

He put the tape in the player, held it up to the phone, and played the song titled, "What Kind of Fool Do You Think I Am?"

He set an emotional boundary with her in no uncertain terms. He had enough sense of himself to feel the pain and to decide for himself, "I'm not doing this again. No, thank you." He wasn't going to volunteer for that kind of abuse again.

WEAK EMOTIONAL BOUNDARIES

If our feelings in childhood were not properly mirrored, allowed, and processed, we were most likely shamed for having them. As a result, we did not develop strong emotional boundaries. Consequently, we have a weak sense of who we are. People who become codependents, writes Ann Wilson Schaef in her book *Co-dependence: Misunderstood-Mistreated*, "take on another's sadness, happiness, fear, or whatever people around them are feeling and/or thinking."[2] If we have a weak sense of ourselves, we will feel what everybody else feels.

When two codependents are in a relationship, their boundaries are fused, Schaef further explains. "This is double codependency." Neither one of them have a sense of self. "If one had a problem, they both had a problem. If one needed a clarification, they both needed a clarification… Each had lost an awareness of the other's boundaries. They were fused."[3]

This enmeshment of emotions creates huge problems in marriages because that's how a codependent defines intimacy. Yet, it has nothing to do with intimacy. It feels close, but it is not close. It is even counter-productive to intimacy. It's saying to the other person, "I am not me, I'm you."

THE AVOIDANCE OF PAIN

If we don't have strong emotional boundaries, we will continue to be the target of abuse and pain. And we will continue to do what we have always done with pain—avoid it. We will do whatever it takes to avoid the pain of abuse.

Scott Peck in his book *The Road Less Traveled* contends that the avoidance of pain is the primary basis of all mental illness.[4] We can make a scale from zero to ten with ten representing that point at which we have totally checked out—in the mental ward staring out the window, wearing a diaper, and spitting up on ourselves. Most of us don't go that far to avoid pain, but we are somewhere on that scale and have created some survival techniques to avoid our pain.

Those of us who are in an abusive situation are preoccupied with survival. We survive until we can escape. The girl gets married at fifteen or sixteen so she can escape the insanity of her abusive home life. "I'm getting out of this house. Dad's an alcoholic. He beats me and he beats Mom, and Mom won't do any thing about it." She may think she is in love with the boy she marries, but in reality she is obsessed with getting out, and he seems like the happy solution.

Since she was not taken through the emotional stages to maturity, and since her survival technique at home was to shut down emotionally, she doesn't know how to have a different relationship from the one that she came out of. As a result, she marries her alcoholic dad in another man. Five alcoholic husbands later, she calls the counseling center, "I need help."

"What's the problem?"

"Well, I've been married five times to the same guy—my dad."

Too often the means that we choose to avoid our pain only increases it.

FEELINGS

If we were abused, we may have employed various means for blocking out painful memories. The feelings, however, don't forget.

We feel things but don't know what those feelings are. We just feel bad. We assume that those feelings must be wrong because they don't line up with what we were told we were supposed to feel and think. We also assume that those bad feelings are our fault because our abuse has told us that we are defective human beings.

We need a feedback system to teach us about our feelings and what they are saying to us.

Feelings are neither good nor bad. Feelings are just feelings. They are visitors that are supposed to tell us something and then go away.

Children feel things but don't know what those feelings are unless someone mirrors them. They need to have their feelings named and validated. They need to know that it is OK for them to have those feelings. They need to learn for themselves what their feelings are.

Sometimes the parent or caretaker needs to provide a menu of feeling names to choose from. Anne was in Bluebirds and didn't want to go to the Bluebird meeting. "I'm not going. Please don't make me go," she protested.

"Sounds like you are angry."

"No, I'm not angry."

"Well, sad? Hurt? Scared?"

"I'm scared. But I don't want to talk about it."

The insensitive parent would argue, "There's nothing to be afraid of. You need to go and you are going."

"I don't want to go."

"You're going and that's it. Get into the car and let's go."

The parent who knows how to mirror and validate Anne's feelings would respond differently. "You're scared? What are you afraid of? Has something happened to you? Come, sit by me and let's talk about this. What happened at Bluebirds that made you afraid?"

"Tony says he's going to hit me if I don't give him my cookies."

Children don't need to hear, "I don't care what you feel. You shouldn't be scared. All good girls go to Bluebird meetings." That message tells the child that neither she nor her feelings matter. She is unable to receive the valuable information that those feelings were supposed to tell her.

When our feelings are accurately mirrored, we get an accurate image of who we are and how we feel. Learning about feelings at an early age is vital to healthy development of an integrated personality. Our thinking, then, lines up with our feelings.

I had tremendous losses in my life as a child. I was an only child—no brothers and sisters. My dad was drunk and gone most of the time. My mother emotionally incested me. The neighbor kids made fun of me. As I look at pictures of me as a little child, I notice I always have a duck, a cat, a rabbit, or a dog in my arms—not stuffed ones, live ones. But even they were a source of loss in my life.

Every time I got a dog it died. If it didn't die naturally, somebody ran over it. When I got a cocker spaniel, it had rabies, so we had to kill it. I had to take shots in the stomach for fourteen weeks. I was given a family of rabbits for Easter one year and my dog ate every one of them; then a truck ran over my dog. I was a sad little guy. Every time I had something close to me it left me.

Proper mirroring for those feeling experiences is to say such things as, "You're sad. I'd be sad, too. I'll bet that hurts. I'll bet you need to cry. I'll cry with you," or "I'll sit with you."

The process of mirroring gives feedback. When feedback from our feelings is accurate, our feelings unfold and become clear. If our feelings continue to be accurately mirrored back to us as we grow up, they become clearer and more accurate, and we are going to be better equipped to handle them. We will be able to learn from our feelings the message they are supposed to send to us. We need to learn how to get in touch with anger, sadness, grief, jealousy—whatever it is. This mirroring is the key to developing a healthy sense of self.

As we continue to get proper mirroring of our feelings as adults, we will come more and more to know who we are, and we will be able to establish more effective boundaries in our lives.

What have you been taught to think and feel about feelings?

When you were growing up, was it OK for you to feel angry, sad, happy—those kinds of feelings?

Was it OK for you to laugh?

Was it OK for you to cry?

What is your attitude toward feelings now?

Feelings determine the nature of our connection to other people.

If we don't know what our feelings are, we are not going to be able to enter into a valid, intimate relationship with another person. You can know what I do. You can know what I look like. You can work with me, live with me, be married to me; but, if I never allow you to know who I am, we can never have an intimate relationship. We cannot know who we are if we are not in touch with our true feelings.

How open are you to sharing your real feelings in your relationships with others, especially with your mate or a significant other?

Are you aware of feelings that you have that others do not know about? What are they?

Why are you afraid for them to know how you feel?

What can you do to be more open in expressing your real feelings?

If we don't set our own boundaries, others will set them for us .

If we don't know what to think, others will do our thinking for us. If we don't know how we feel, others will tell us how they want us to feel or not feel. And that's who we become. "I'm not who *I* think I am. I'm not even who *you* think I am. *I am* who *I* think *you* think I am."

When we try to set some realistic goals based on what *we* really want and need, we have difficulty identifying our needs. We are more able to identify the needs of others. We know what Mama wanted. We know what the children need. We know the car needs fixing. But what do *we* really want? We don't know because we are out of touch with what we want and need for ourselves.

Our boundaries have been trespassed by other people who have deposited things about themselves upon us and taken away things about us. And we think that is who we are.

When our boundaries are vague to us, they will be vague to others. "Can I borrow your chain saw?" We say *yes* but in our minds we really don't want to loan out our chain saw. A month later, no chain saw. We're murmuring to ourselves, "I'm gonna get that guy if he doesn't bring my chain saw back." We end up having to go get the saw ourselves because a tree has fallen in our backyard. The blade is dull. The engine is burned up because he didn't add oil to it. We end up resenting him, but we would never let him know that we resent him because we don't want this guy not to like us. He might think we are selfish.

How has someone else in your life set boundaries for you that you really didn't want?

Do you let others tell you what to think and/or how to feel?

As best as you can, list your emotional needs.

THOUGHTS AND FEELINGS

There is a difference between thoughts and feelings. Oftentimes when we are asked what we "feel" about something, we express our thoughts and not our feelings. Think about having gone out to eat with your closest friends. Your best friend said that she would be there, but never showed. She told you she fell asleep and didn't wake up in time. However, you later found out that she went to a movie with someone else but didn't want you to know about it. Now you are asked what you feel about that. If you answer, "she lied to me." That's a thought statement. If you said, "I'm hurt and angry to think that she would lie to me." That's a feeling statement. Hurt and anger are feeling words.

Examples of other feeling words are *rejected, insecure, fearful, perplexed, curious, excited, happy, playful, grateful, sad, lonely, depressed, nervous, exhausted, bitter, frustrated, anxious, jealous, disgusted, horrified, and grieved.*

Think of a recent boundary violation and list the feelings you had when the violation occurred.

Do you still have the same feelings about the incident?

HOW WE VIOLATE EMOTIONAL BOUNDARIES

Here are some of the typical ways we can violate emotional boundaries:

A violation of emotional boundaries occurs when we are either too intrusive or too distant.

An intrusive violation occurs when someone goes beyond the emotional limits that are appropriate to the relationship. Janie didn't feel good about herself and was vulnerable to any male compliment that was paid her. Brad, a near stranger to her, told her how attractive he thought she was. He quickly picked up on her vulnerability to his flattery and continued his phony compliments. He used this flattery to play on her need for acceptance which led to a sexual encounter with him. This may not have happened had Janie been able to set healthy boundaries.

A distancing violation occurs when someone fails to provide the appropriate emotional intimacy expected in that relationship. Lillian was needing a hug from her husband. Bill was too involved working on his computer project. "Not now, honey, can't you see that I'm busy?" A few seconds away from the project would have meant a lot to the relationship. Instead, his insensitivity took away from it—Bill's response sent Lillian the message that his project was more important to him than she was.

Withholding intimacy from children in the family is a distancing boundary violation that damages the child emotionally and produces a child without boundaries. Four-year-old Daniel raced over to Dad to give him a goodnight hug and kiss. Dad picked him up, said, "Good night," but never made eye-to-eye contact with him because he was more interested in Monday night football on TV. Thirty minutes later Dad turned to Mom. "Where's the kid?"

"You don't remember? He came in and gave you a goodnight hug and kiss and went to bed."

"Oh, yeah. I remember," he says as he flips through the channels looking for something else to watch during half-time.

Anne Katherine points out that both physical and emotional boundaries are harmed by either intrusive or distancing violations. She notes that distancing violations during developmental years have one of two results: Because we never learned to connect, we either become loners who are unable to let anyone come close, or we have such an inner void that we fill ourselves with the identity of someone else. In either case, we are emotionally violated.[5]

How have you been emotionally violated by someone who was too emotionally intrusive?

How have you been emotionally violated by someone who was too emotionally distant?

How have you been emotionally intrusive and to whom?

How have you been emotionally distant and to whom?

What choices can you begin to make to avoid future intrusive or distancing violations?

A violation of emotional boundaries occurs when we do not provide proper mirroring of our children's feelings during their formative years.

It is the parents' responsibility to guide their children toward emotional health and stability through proper mirroring of their children's feelings during the formative years.

If, as children, our feelings were not properly mirrored, it was a direct violation against us and sets us up to be emotional violators ourselves. Without proper mirroring, we will grow up with an identity crisis, our emotional maturity will be stymied, and we will not know how to have intimate relationships with others. We will be ill-equipped to deal with many issues in adult life. We will not be able to tell when we are being abused, neither will we know when our own emotional behavior is inappropriate.

Abused children often dissociate from their feelings. In extreme cases of abuse, the child dissociates to the point of developing alter personalities in order to cope.

A violation of emotional boundaries occurs when we enmesh with others.

Enmeshment is when one person's life and feelings take over those of another person. Enmeshment occurs at various levels in our system of relationships.

Parent to child. Frank and Mary have been married twelve years and have a nine-year-old daughter named Sarah. Frank is an alcoholic. He is emotionally and physically unavailable to the family. He goes fishing and drinking with his buddies but rarely does anything with the family. He always has an excuse for his absence. He is not meeting Mary's needs sexually, emotionally, or relationally. She cooks dinner, and he comes in late and passes out on the couch.

Mary feels abandoned after all these years. She can't bear the thought of Frank touching her. He's drunk all the time. He doesn't know about intimacy, but he sure knows about sex. She feels violated by him sexually.

This is a dysfunctional family. Dad has a relationship with his alcohol. This whole family has a relationship with the disease of alcoholism. They have unhealthy and non-nurturing relationships with one another.

Mary uses little Sarah to meet her emotional needs. In so doing, she becomes emotionally enmeshed with Sarah. This is also called emotional incest. The real Sarah has been smothered out by who mother is. She has become an extension of her mother and is conditioned to be what her mother needs from her.

So, we have an emotionally distant parent in Frank and an emotionally intrusive parent in Mary.

When Frank misses Sarah's school play, Mary clings to little Sarah saying, "I'll go to your play. We'll be there together—just you and me. We'll be buddies. When you grow up and leave home, I just don't know what I will do."

The unspoken message Mary communicates to Sarah is this: "Your Dad is never around for me, either. I'll depend upon you to be there for Mommy. I need you to meet my needs." In reality, Mom is not going to the play for Sarah, but is going in order to have her own needs met.

Sarah grew up with no boundaries because her own boundaries were violated. It became her job in adulthood to meet everyone else's needs. She was not allowed to have needs of her own, and if she should have them, it was not OK for anyone else to meet those needs. She became a classic caretaker.

Dad has his own version of emotional abuse. After all, his wife has cut him off. He is sexually needy and doesn't have his wife to meet that need. To whom does he turn? Little Sarah! "Come here, honey, give your Daddy a big hug." Even if it is an appropriate hug, the emotional exchange is now meeting his needs instead of giving Sarah the kind of hug that meets her needs.

Nine-year-old Sarah has to meet the needs of both parents. They are sapping the child of everything she has. The problem is she doesn't have anything to give except the garbage they have been dumping into her. Garbage in, garbage out.

If Sarah shows any resistance to affection, they heap guilt and shame on top of the garbage they've dumped into her. "What's the matter, honey, don't you love Daddy anymore?"

Kids are like little garbage cans in dysfunctional families. The parents walk up, lift the top off of their little persons, and dump all of their feelings into them. They put their anger, resentments, hate, lusts, and habits in there. Then they put the lid back on the garbage can. When little Sarah started snorting cocaine and became sexually active at the age of thirteen, they were shocked with disbelief. Yet, Sarah was only playing out the garbage that was dumped into her.

Enmeshment creates stress in a child that is carried over into adulthood. Kirk came for counseling after he suffered a severe panic attack. It gradually became apparent that he was under a great deal of stress. He eventually saw how his grandmother, who practically raised him, had violated his boundaries by enmeshment. She was intrusive. His mother, on the other hand, violated him by not being there for him hardly at all. She was too distant. He found himself working very hard to please both of them. It should never have been his job to meet either of their needs.

In the case of Kirk's grandmother, she had needs that no one else was available to meet. She chose him to meet her needs, and thereby placed unrealistic expectations on him. Kirk was unable to meet those needs and began to withdraw from her. His withdrawal was threatening to her, and she manipulated him all the more to try to keep him connected. The manipulation produced guilt and shame in Kirk. He internalized this tension. On the one hand, he felt he "ought" to meet her needs but, on the other hand, was unable to emotionally carry that load any longer. This tension from childhood and youth was at least one of the hidden psychological sources for his panic.

A child who has been emotionally incested is a "used child"—used to meet the parent's needs.

In her book, *The Emotional Incest Syndrome*, Dr. Patricia Love describes four types of parents who enmesh with their children, "the Romanticizing Parent, the Neglectful Parent, the Critical/Abusive Parent, and the Sexualizing Parent."[6]

Romanticizing Parents are those who turn to their children of the opposite sex for intimacy and companionship that is not appropriate for the relationship. This is called surrogate spousing because the children are taking the place of the other spouse in meeting certain needs. These parents have undue adoration for their children. Closely akin to this are the parents who become "best friends" or "buddies" to their children of the same sex. This occurs mostly with single parents and when there is only one child in the family.[7]

Neglectful Parents abdicate their role as parents. They abandon their children so that the children must take responsibility for themselves beyond their natural ability to do so. Therapists call these "parentified children." They have to learn to feed and clothe themselves and make many other decisions about themselves that should have been made for them. This forces them to "grow up" before their years. Consequently, they do not "grow up" properly but have a thwarted perspective on maturity. Children of alcoholic parents may suffer both extremes. They are neglected when those parents are drunk and smothered when they are sober.

Critical/Abusive Parents are hypercritical of their children. They say things to them and treat them in ways that make them feel like failures. They can never perform well enough. The children who are drawn in too close by one parent will become the targets of jealousy and meanness by the other parent. The children are used for the release of anger and tension by the Critical/Abusive Parent. Whatever emotion these parents are feeling are dumped on these children. "Domestic violence, poverty, alcoholism, drug abuse, or criminal activity may also be part of the picture," Dr. Love writes. "These more obvious problems mask the enmeshment. Many people who were raised by physically abusive or alcoholic parents, for example, belatedly discover that they were also the victims of emotional incest."[8]

Sexualizing Parents are those whose sexual cups are not being filled by their mates so they turn to one of their children and enmesh with them. Dad turns to the daughter and Mom turns to the son. They may engage in sexual incest, but it is not limited to that. Such parents may pay more attention than normal to the child in general. They may touch, hug, or kiss the child inappropriately. They may show unhealthy interest in their children's bodies, invade their privacy in the bedroom or bathroom, take pornographic pictures or videos of them, use sexual and seductive language with them. These parents fail to set appropriate limits for their children and expose them to experiences beyond their years.

Dr. Love calls the emotionally incested child the "Chosen Child." She suggests that the adult Chosen Child will deny that there were any problems in the family. This denial is further clouded by the "collection of lies, evasions, distortions, and half-truths designed to obscure an unpleasant reality."[9]

Moreover, the adult Chosen Child will suffer from a sense of guilt, chronic low-level anxiety, fluctuating self-esteem, fear of rejection, social isolation, a feeling of inferiority, denial of his own needs, a compulsive need to succeed, a diffused sense of identity, an inability to separate from the parent, personal boundary problems, fear of commitment, lack of romantic attraction, conflict between the spouse and the parent, attraction to self-centered partners, and sexual problems.[10]

The following fill-in-the-blank statements, adapted from a checklist by Dr. Love, are indicators of enmeshment.[11] They are signs of an involvement that is way out of bounds. If you were truly enmeshed, they will apply in your situation. However, any one of us may be able to identify with some of these statements to one extent or another. If you were not emotionally enmeshed, few of these statements will apply to you.

Write in the name of the parent that fits the statements. If stepparents, grandparents, and other significant caretakers apply, write in their names instead. If you need to write other kinds of responses such as "this was true before mother (or daddy) remarried (or died)," then do so. Include other thoughts, feelings, and observations you may have. Fill in only those statements that apply to your particular situation.

This first set of statements indicate an overly close parent-child bond:

I felt the closest to _____.

118

I was a source of emotional support for _____.

I was _____'s best friend.

_____ shared confidential things with me.

_____ was deeply involved in my activities or in developing my talents.

_____took a lot of pride in my abilities or achievements.

_____ gave me special privileges or gifts.

_____ told me in confidence that I was the favorite, most talented, or most lovable child.

_____ told me I was better company than his or her spouse.

I sometimes felt guilty when I spent time away from _____.

_____ did not want me to marry or move far away from home.

I idolized _____ when I was young.

Any potential boyfriend or girlfriend of mine was never "good enough" for _____.

_____ made inappropriate sexual remarks or violated my privacy.

This second set of statements indicate the unmet needs of the adult parent/caretaker in your life:
My parents were separated, divorced, widowed, or didn't get along very well.   Yes_____   No_____

_____was often lonely, angry, or depressed.

_____did not have a lot of friends.

_____had a drinking or drug problem.

_____thought the other parent was too indulgent or permissive.

I felt I had to hold back my own needs to protect _____ .

_____turned to me for comfort and or advice.

_____ seemed to rely on me more than on my siblings.

I felt responsible for _____'s happiness.

My parents disagreed about parenting issues.   Yes____   No____

This third set of statements indicate parental neglect or abuse:
My needs were often ignored or neglected.   Yes____   No____

There was a great deal of conflict between me and _____.

_____ called me hurtful names.

_____ had unrealistic expectations of me.

I sometimes wanted to hide from _____ or had fantasies of running away.

When I was a child other families seemed less emotionally intense than mine.   Yes____   No____

It was often a relief to get away from home.   Yes____   No____

I sometimes felt invaded by _____ .

I sometimes felt I added to _____'s unhappiness.

Dr. Love suggests that if you identified with ten or more of the above statements, there is a likelihood that enmeshment occurred to some degree. If you identified with most of the statements in the first two groups, she suggests that the enmeshment was with a Romanticizing or Sexual Parent. If you identified mostly with statements in the last two groups, you have been enmeshed with a Critical/Abusive Parent. If you identified with a sprinkling of statements throughout the three groups, "you may have been alternately loved and abused by the same parent, or one parent may have abused you while the other adored you," she writes.[12]

Vicarious living. Living vicariously through our children to fulfill our own failed dreams is a form of enmeshment. The boy is going to be that football player that Dad never was. So he grooms him, shames him, guilt-provokes him, beats him, hammers him, and molds him into being the star player.
"Well, Dad, I really would rather take piano lessons."
"Oh, no. My son plays football. Now get out there and kill somebody today."

"But I hate football, Dad. It hurts."

But in order to get approval from Dad, he plays football.

Mother preps the daughter to be the beauty queen Mom never got to be. By the time daughter is five years old, her mother has her competing in beauty contests with a view to the Miss America pageant.

Were you the victim of vicarious living?

What measures can you take to be who you are and fulfill your own goals rather than those of another?

How can you insure that you will not live your life vicariously through someone else?

Marital enmeshment. Enmeshment is not only parent to child. It frequently happens between husbands and wives and other relationships as well.

Anne Katherine says an ideal marriage contains the necessary togetherness to preserve our boundaries yet allows enough separation to preserve our individuality. "It's critical for each person to have his and her own thoughts and feelings, and for each to take responsibility for his or her own actions."[13]

Sometimes we repeat what we see our parents doing as they relate to one another, and sometimes we do the opposite to avoid what we perceive as their mistakes. Therefore, the following questions are asked about your parents and also about yourself and your spouse or another with whom you are in a significant relationship. If your circumstances warrant, you may want to apply the "partner" questions to a previous relationship.

These questions are adapted from Dr. Love's lists of ten roles and responsibilities of adult partners.[14]

Did your parents respect and support each other?

Do you and your partner respect and support each other?

Did your parents nurture each other?

Do you and your partner nurture each other?

Did your parents practice tolerance?

Do you and your partner practice tolerance?

Did your parents have fun together?

Do you and your partner have fun together?

Were your parents lovers?

Are you and your partner lovers?

Did your parents share significant interests?

Do you and your partner share significant interests?

Were your parents confidants?

Are you and your partner confidants?

Were your parents financial partners?

Are you and your partner financial partners?

Were your parents the primary social partner of one another?

Are you and your partner the primary social partner of one another?

Did your parents resolve conflicts and work out problems?

Do you and your partner resolve conflicts and work out problems?

The next two questions indicate possible enmeshment.
Did one of your parents always speak or answer for the other one?

Do you or your partner always speak or answer for the other one?

Based on all of your answers above, would you say that your parents had a responsible and healthy relationship?

What can you do to strengthen your relationship with your partner?

A violation of emotional boundaries occurs when we are shamed.

Typically, if we were abused as children, we may have emotional problems, night terrors, fears, abandonment issues, rage—feelings we don't know how to process.

Feelings are visitors with a message. They are supposed to visit us, tell us a message, then they are supposed to go away.

However we invite them in. "Oh, come on in. I have a hidden room down inside. There's a bunch of other guys, and you'll be right at home." So, we bury those feelings.

The problem is, we bury them alive. They don't die. While they're down in there, they eat and we keep feeding them. They get bigger. We get into counseling and somebody says, "You need to get in touch with your feelings." We get in touch with them, all right. We open that closet door and an army of feelings march out to devour everyone in sight.

John Bradshaw teaches that feelings are energy in motion. They have to go somewhere. He says that shame is the master emotion.[15] It whips all the rest of the emotions into shape. When we come from a dysfunctional family background where we were taught that it was not OK to feel, shame is given the power to keep the other feelings in check.

We can have healthy shame or toxic shame. If we do something wrong, our conscience tells us that we are guilty and we will probably feel ashamed. That's healthy. Healthy shame tells us that we made a mistake. Toxic shame tells us we *are* a mistake. It says that we are a defective unit even when we haven't done anything wrong.

The verbal expressions we speak over our children can curse and shame them for life—those "always" and "never" statements. "You *always* do it wrong. You *never* do anything right." These repeated curses script the child's entire life if he or she does not get help.

We don't get all of our shame from home, however. We can get shamed in any of our systems of relationships: neighbors, playmates, schoolmates, church members, coworkers.

We can be addicted to shame just as we can be addicted to any form of abuse we suffer. We may even get a "high" off of the shame and the abuse. It is similar to an adrenaline rush. We are compelled to do things that produce this shame. Even though it is toxic shame, we subconsciously live to feel it. Shame seems to make us feel good for being bad. It's our dues, our payment for sin. We think if we feel the shame, we will be able to cover our evilness. Of course, this is all a lie. The shame actually drives us to commit more and greater boundary violations.

Here are some of the ways we are shamed:

Improper Mirroring. We are shamed when our emotions are not properly mirrored.

Caretakers will either mirror their children's feelings to help them develop a sense of who they are, or they will shame those feelings and encourage the creation of false selves.

Dad yells at his four-year-old son who fall and hurts himself. "Don't be a crybaby. Get up and take it like a man." This statement and attitude from Dad shames the boy for falling, shames him for having pain, shames him for crying, and shames him for being a four-year-old instead of an adult man. It denies him the right to be a little boy in that moment. It leaves the boy confused: "I'm hurt, but I'm not supposed to be hurt. I don't get it."

Performance. We are shamed when we fail to accomplish demands put upon us that are beyond our ability to perform.

From the time I was a child, I have always had to have a bowl of cereal before bedtime. One night I started to the kitchen and realized that I wasn't even hungry. Why did I have to have that cereal? I was surprised when I remembered myself as a little boy in our house down on Main Street. I was in the early grades. I had been given homework but didn't know how to do it. I was expected to get it done, but there wasn't anyone who could show me how to do it. I felt fearful and anxious because I knew I would be shamed the next day at school for not having my homework finished. So, I would eat a bowl of cereal with sugar and milk to medicate my feelings. The sugar and the milk still pacify me. –CEN

Verbal Abuse. We are shamed when we are persistently teased, belittled, or verbally attacked.

I grew up with people making rude comments to me. I was a skinny, bucktoothed, freckle-faced, red-headed kid who was the last guy to get picked on every team. I was the guy at the end about whom they would say, "All right, we'll give you two more guys if you take O'Neil." Girls couldn't stand me. I wore high-top, brown, corrective shoes until I was in the second grade. I couldn't wear tennis shoes, and I was knocked-kneed.

School was a torture chamber for me so far as my peers were concerned. Bullies picked on me. At my birthday party when I was seven years old, a bully came down on my block. He smarted off to me in front of all my friends, and I said something back to him. We ended up in a fight—in a mud hole. The bully beat me up at my own party in front of all my friends. I had mud in my ears and eyes, and I felt awful. I was shamed and teased unmercifully. I know now that those comments were not about me. They were about the others making the comments. But I didn't understand that then.

How did you experience shame growing up? Think of parents, siblings, school mates, friends, teachers, religious people and experiences.

How were you shamed for your failure to perform beyond your ability to do so?

What kind of things have been said about you persistently that belittles you or makes you feel attacked?

How are you shaming others?

What boundaries can you set to safeguard against further shaming experiences?

A violation of emotional boundaries occurs when authorities think they have the right to say or do anything they want.

Violations that occur when the limits of a role are ignored, forgotten or over-stepped have an emotional impact on us. Fathers may enslave their children to chores that rob them of their childhood. The boss may require unmerciful hours and unrealistic achievement. The teacher may demand homework involving time beyond reason. These infractions injure us emotionally.

How can you safeguard yourself from emotional boundary violations from authorities?

How can you avoid violating a subordinate's emotional boundaries?

A violation of emotional boundaries occurs when we overprotect and, thereby, shame the individuality of the one being overly protected.

When we are overprotected, we get a message that we are inadequate or incapable of taking care of ourselves. It is especially damaging on males because men get their significance from successfully doing things. The inability of a male to perform makes him feel that he is a defective person.

If Mom is the one who has overprotected him, he is likely to grow up, go out, and find a dominating female to marry who will take care of things for him and fight his battles for him.

A mother confessed to overprotecting her firstborn son. "I have hovered over this child from the day he was born. He is so overwrought with fear that he is going to be as damaged as I have been. He won't try anything. He whines, 'I can't. You have to do it for me. I can't tie my shoes. I can't draw a letter. I can't, I can't, I can't.' I'm trying to encourage him. I realized that he had a problem, but I didn't realize until now that I had caused it."

It is hard to turn those kinds of patterns around. This mom needed to allow her son to figure out the solutions to his own problems. She could be available on the sidelines to encourage him and show him how to do things, but not to do them for him.

How were you overprotected?

What life consequences do you think this has had upon you?

How are you overprotecting others?

What boundaries can you set to safeguard against overprotection?

A violation of emotional boundaries occurs when we commit emotional infidelity.

Relationships exist in part to provide emotional support for one another. Different levels of support apply to different levels of relationships. Husbands and wives are supposed to provide emotional support for each other. Parents are supposed to provide emotional support for their children. There is a level at which persons may receive appropriate emotional support from their ministers, from their therapists, or within their support groups. Colleagues at work can be supportive of each other in times of crises.

Emotional infidelity occurs when a certain type of support is sought from or given to another person who is inappropriately chosen for that support. The man or the woman who finds emotional support in a personal, intimate relationship outside of the marriage is guilty of emotional infidelity.

"My wife doesn't understand me."

"My husband is never there for me."

These are seductive statements, especially if they are made to another party who may already have some romantic interest, and especially if the other party is a caretaker.

These may be true statements. But there are appropriate and constructive alternatives to take before we allow ourselves to get emotionally involved with another person.

Some people find that emotional transference outside of the marriage is more threatening and damaging than sexual infidelity. Sex addicts don't have sex in order to have relationships. They have sex just like an alcoholic has a drink—strictly for the buzz. Although sex is an intimacy issue, sex alone does not constitute intimacy. Emotional infidelity is an intimacy issue.

How have you been the victim of emotional infidelity?

How did it affect you?

How have you been a perpetrator of emotional infidelity and against whom?

What boundaries can you set to safeguard against emotional infidelity?

A violation of emotional boundaries occurs when we dump our rage upon others, especially our children.

Not only have the children of non-nurturing families not had their feelings properly mirrored, they have had the feelings of their parents dumped on them as well. We, as adult children of dysfunction, get into therapy and discover that not all of those things we feel are our feelings. We think we are supposed to have these feelings because that's all we ever felt growing up. Although we are sure to have our own measure of rage for ourselves, most of it may not be ours. It's our dad's or our mom's.

We carry that rage around inside of us regardless of whose it is. We are the ones who have been and are continuing to be violated by it. That rage within us greatly affects our lives.

Check the following sentences that best describe your typical response when confronted by another's rage.

___I will withdraw and shut down.

___I will deny the charge even if it is true because I can't handle correction.

___I will lie about the truth to make myself look good.

___I will side-track the issue.

___I will try to make it the other person's fault.

___I will try to be humorous.

___I will go out and use something to make me feel better (sex, alcohol, drugs, work, or any number of addictive behaviors).

___I will rationalize or intellectualize.

___I will get angry, call names, and threaten.

___I will manipulate by being cold.

___I will manipulate by sweet-talking.

___I will show excessive concern for the other person.

___I will listen and admit to my fault.

___I will apologize for my honest mistakes.

___I will apologize even if it is not my fault.

BEING RESPONSIBLE

As adults, we are responsible for our feelings and for how we act out those feelings. Responsibility and maturity involves getting in touch with our feelings and doing the right things regardless of our feelings. We may be very angry but that doesn't mean we can get an AK-47 and wipe out McDonalds. We don't always have to "do" something with our feelings. Feelings don't necessarily reflect reality. Oftentimes they reflect everything but reality. That's why we need a mentor or mature friend who can keep us in reality.

It's not too late to establish healthy emotional boundaries. If we want to get well and grow emotionally, we are going to have to get in touch with our feelings and set new boundaries accordingly. We need to line up our thinking with our feelings and get honest with ourselves. The combination of effective feedback and knowing ourselves better creates an emotional boundary.

Write a brief summary of what you learned about yourself as you answered these questions. What thoughts, feelings, and attitudes surfaced or became more clear to you?

Based on what you have learned in this chapter, summarize the new healthy boundaries you can begin to exercise in your relationships.

GROUP EXPERIENCE

Group Leader:

1. Ask if there are any questions about the information in this chapter. Allow others to answer through group discussion.

2. Have the group to identify the types of emotional boundary violations mentioned in the text (intrusion, distancing, improper mirroring, enmeshment, shaming, misuse of authority, overprotection, emotional infidelity, and raging). List these on a chalkboard.

Ask someone to pick one of these types of violations and direct a reenactment of their personal experience of abuse in that area.

Walk the person back through the situation, slowing down the action, and talk about how it could have been handled in a safer and more appropriate way. Ask the group to tell what things stood out the most to them as they saw the reenactment.

Repeat the process with other examples of emotional abuse.

3. Divide the group into pairs and ask them to share their answers from this chapter that were most significant to them. Also have them tell how they are doing with any new boundaries that they have begun to exercise and evaluate with one another any additional boundaries they have decided to set.

4. Bring the group back together to discuss final questions, thoughts, and feelings.

Set time limits on these group sessions. Remind them that they do not have to share anything they are not ready to share.

— 13 —

Models of Unhealthy Boundaries

FUNCTIONAL AND RELATIONAL BOUNDARIES

"*Functional boundaries*," according to Henry Cloud and John Townsend, "refers to a person's ability to complete a task, project, or job." They have "to do with such things as performance, discipline, initiative, and planning."[1] Functional boundaries apply mostly in work and task-oriented situations.

When we fail to perform our functions as we should, we violate the boundaries of others. Harriet asked her new friend, Bob, to paint the trim around her house. Bob asked for and received the money up front, failed to complete the job, and did a poor job of what he did complete. He never repaid the money. Harriet had to hire someone else to finish the job and it cost her much more than it should have. Harriet opened herself to abuse by paying the full price before the job was completed. Bob violated Harriet by his negligent performance on the job.

"*Relational boundaries* refers to the ability to speak truth to others with whom we are in a relationship," writes Cloud and Townsend.[2] The person who has extra loads of work dumped on him and can't say *no* because he is a compliant type person also won't truthfully tell the other person how he feels about it. If we are the type to avoid trouble in relationships, we'll do our work, then we'll eat your lunch later on.

Some people have great functional boundaries. They can do their human-doing kinds of things, but they have no relational boundaries. Other people have great relational boundaries, but can't get anything done.

We love hanging out with Bob, so we hire him. "Where's the report, Bob?"

"I don't know, man, let's hang out. Boy, we really have a great relationship haven't we?"

"Yea, Bob, but the report."

"Oh yeah, the report, I'll get to that. Let's talk about how we feel."

Knowing the difference between functional and relational boundaries will enable you to evaluate the areas in which your boundaries need to be improved.

How might you improve upon your functional boundaries (consider discipline, initiative, and planning ahead)?

How might you improve upon your relational boundaries?

Boundaries are all about relationships to persons and things. Our relationships are either healthy, nourishing, and functional; or unhealthy, non-nourishing, and dysfunctional. Boundaries are unhealthy and dysfunctional when they are too close or too distant, too rigid or too flexible, too permeable or too impermeable.[3] Examine the following models of unhealthy boundaries and determine which of these most accurately apply to you. None of us have boundaries that are always one way or the other. We may have some boundaries that are too flexible while others are too rigid. We may even have a few normal, healthy boundaries along the way. Be as honest with yourself as you can.

BOUNDARIES THAT ARE TOO CLOSE

People with boundaries that are too close allow people into their lives beyond what is needful and appropriate. They have difficulty knowing when a matter is none of the other person's business. Consequently, they do not have a clear sense of privacy either in space, thoughts, or feelings. They think they have to allow everyone they meet into their lives.

People with boundaries that are too close, likewise, tend to bring others into their lives closer than others want to be or should be. They tell people things that others have no interest in knowing.

The server informs the dinner party that the soup of the day is broccoli-cheese. "Oh, I can't have that," the too-close person says to the server. "I have to watch my cholesterol level and intake of saturated fats. I had by-pass surgery last year and I'm on a strict diet." The server could care less.

Anne Katherine calls these "leaky boundaries." She says that parents with leaky boundaries tell their children more than they need to know. This makes the children feel they are responsible for things they should not be responsible for. They grow up feeling overly responsible on the one hand, but inadequate to meet those responsibilities on the other hand.[4]

If a woman with boundaries that are too close marries a man with boundaries that are too distant, she is setting herself up for major problems in the marriage. Her energy will be spent on trying to draw in her resistant, distant, avoidant, non-responsive husband.

"He won't talk to me. I don't know how he feels. We've been married for fourteen years and I don't even know who he is."

The more one tries to get close to the distant person, the further away the distant person is driven. "Give me a break, woman. I can't breathe."

The mate who has boundaries that are too close will be vulnerable to the mood changes of the spouse with the too distant boundaries. He or she may do too much and take over jobs that belong to the spouse.

Who do you know that talks too much, telling others far more than they want to hear or should hear?

How have you victimized others by telling them more information than they need to know?

How have you been the victim of a person with boundaries that are too close?

What choices can you make to safeguard against boundaries that are too close?

BOUNDARIES THAT ARE TOO DISTANT

People with boundaries that are too distant don't allow people into their lives for what is needful and appropriate. The person with boundaries that are too distant is isolated, has trouble making friends, and can't express his feelings even to the people he should be able to trust. He neglects those for whom he has responsibility.

Mates with distant boundaries will have difficulty connecting with their spouse. They will have poor contact with their own feelings and be unable to communicate them. They may interpret affection and interest as intrusive or prying. Just a friendly gesture may seem intrusive and smothering.

The same is true of the parents who are emotionally unavailable to their children. The children of the distant parent will experience "insufficient affection and healthy touching, abandonment, and the fear that comes from not feeling connected to the caregiver in power," writes Katherine.[5]

Boundaries that are too distant equals neglect. Neglect is abuse.

How have you been the victim of a person with boundaries that are too distant?

How have you victimized others by distancing yourself from them?

What choices can you make to safeguard against boundaries that are too distant?

BOUNDARIES THAT ARE TOO CLOSE AND TOO DISTANT

People with boundaries that are too close and too distant have a come-here, go-away mentality. Parents can be too close and too distant with their children. They want to be close to the child, and are in ways that smother the child, but they do not allow the child to come close to them. These parents need emotional support from the child but are ill-equipped to give it. They need the child's approval. "What are you thinking, Jenny?" "Do you love mommy?" Katherine claims that this is an invasion of the child's space. The parents demand that the child think and feel a certain way.[6]

Husbands and wives can be too close and too distant as well. One of the mates can be particularly needy—always needing the attention of the other mate but unable to give. He or she may be close one moment, giving a message of intimacy, and turn distant the next. This makes the other mate crazy.

This boundary issue has a subtle mix of feelings which says, "I want to be close, but I'm afraid to be close." Or, "I want you to be close, but I am afraid for you to be close."

How have you been victimized by boundaries that were too close and too distant?

How have you victimized others with boundaries that are too close and too distant?

What choices can you make to safeguard against boundaries that are too close and too distant?

BOUNDARIES THAT ARE TOO RIGID

Persons with boundaries that are too rigid are set in their ways. Anne Katherine says they only see life one way. They can't receive new ideas and experiences or discuss matters outside of their field of vision.[7] "My mind is all made up, don't confuse me with the facts." "This is the way things are, get used to it." "This is the only way we can relate to each other." They are entrapped within their own rigid boundaries.

Such persons are legalistic and intolerant of others. There is little room for doubt, correction, or acceptance of others whose ideas and ways are different from their own.

Parents whose boundaries are too rigid have numerous strict rules for their children. Any slight infraction by the children triggers rage from the parent. "Don't cry or you will have to go to your room without dinner!" "You didn't finish your homework by suppertime, so you're grounded for a week!" "You didn't cut the grass like I told you to, so you can't play in your ball game tonight!"

After three days of rain the stir-crazy kids were begging to go outside and play. "No," mother said. "Absolutely not. You'll get wet."

"Can't we just take a walk down the block?"

"No."

"Well, what if we stay on the driveway?"

"I said, 'No!' Go to your room and don't ask me again!"

Children with parents who are too rigid grow up not knowing how to play and have a good time. The spontaneity and creativity of childhood is stifled.

Nine-year-old Mark went with his perfectionist father to settle a discipline problem at school. The school counselor asked Mark's father what his expectations were. Dad dogmatically reacted, "I was brought up to be perfect; I expect my son to be perfect; and, by George, he's going to be." At present sighting, little Mark was "perfect." He was a "perfect" little monster—acting out rebellion against a boundary that was too rigid and impossible to live up to. Mark had no chance of emerging into his own unique self, but was being molded by Dad's high, unrealistic expectations of him.

The working wife of a too rigid husband comes into the room, "Honey, I'm tired of cooking. I've worked all day. I can't cook every night like this. I would like to try out other arrangements. Maybe we could go out somewhere or maybe you could take turns with me in the kitchen."

He responds, "You shouldn't feel that way. We've been married ten years and you've been cooking dinner every night. What's changed? You were working when we first got married; I don't see any reason why you can't come home and cook dinner like you always have."

He is not open to acknowledging her feelings or helping resolve her burn-out.

How were you the victim of someone else's boundaries that were too rigid?

How are you victimizing another with boundaries that are too rigid?

What choices can you make to safeguard against boundaries that are too rigid?

BOUNDARIES THAT ARE TOO FLEXIBLE

People with boundaries that are too flexible are like chameleons. They change their colors to blend into others around them and hide their own individuality. They are too accommodating. They stick their finger in the air to see which way the wind is blowing and change to please everyone they can. They drive themselves and everyone else crazy because it is virtually impossible to please everyone.

Katherine characterizes these kinds of people as being overwhelmed with life.

They are disorganized and easily distracted by new demands put upon them.

They have trouble setting priorities and following them which makes them untrustworthy and irritating to be around.

They are unable to make choices. They may not even be able to choose a partner or spouse.

They may marry someone just because that person asked them instead of because they wanted to.

They are easily manipulated into relationships.

They have no sense of their own preferences.

They are forgetful.

They allow others to get too close to them and do things that are inappropriate. Bill makes advances to Judy and Judy's boundaries are too flexible. She's feeling (not particularly thinking it), "I really need to say 'no,' and I don't need to do this. But I don't want you to not like me." When confronted about it, "I don't really know what happened. It just happened." This is classic addictive behavior. Our addictions rob us of our power of choice. When someone comes along and our boundaries are too flexible, we give in without making a conscious choice to do so.

People with boundaries that are too flexible are overly responsive to others.

They bring constant disorder into their lives and homes. Matt calls home at four o'clock to say he will be home for dinner at six. He shows up at nine, explaining that some of the guys wanted to play handball after work. His boundaries weren't strong enough to say, "My wife is looking for me to be home at six." There was no consideration given to call his wife back and tell her that he had a change of plans. He wonders why she's losing it and he's losing her.

People with boundaries that are too flexible raise children who feel a lack of security. These children won't know how to set clear limits and standards for themselves. They will grow up selfish and unable to respect the needs of others. They will feel unimportant and abandoned. Parents with boundaries that are too flexible are easily manipulated by their children which gives their children too much power.[8]

How were you the victim of boundaries that were too flexible?

How are you victimizing others with boundaries that are too flexible?

What choices can you make to safeguard against boundaries that are too flexible?

BOUNDARIES THAT ARE TOO PERMEABLE

Healthy boundaries allow persons to move back and forth through each other's lives as is appropriate for the relationship. People with boundaries that are too permeable allow other people to penetrate their lives and space more than is appropriate for the relationship.

Parents who missed having a childhood of their own often want to escape the responsibility of adulthood. They try to relive their childhood by identifying too closely with the lives of their children. They permeate their children's boundaries. This often leads to enmeshment. Children who are raised in this environment have difficulty developing a sense of who they are and will take on the attitudes, interests, and goals of another person, such as their mate, as though these things were their own. And they grow up with boundaries that are too permeable.

Take Dan, for example. People walk into his life and think it's OK to dump all of their problems on him. Dan gives them that message because he doesn't know it's not OK for them to do so. He makes everyone's problems his own, therefore he feels responsible to fix them. He attracts self-centered people into his life who use and abuse him.

How were you victimized by boundaries that were too permeable?

How have you victimized others because their boundaries were too permeable?

What choices can you make to safeguard against boundaries that are too permeable?

BOUNDARIES THAT ARE TOO IMPERMEABLE

People with boundaries that are too impermeable do not permit others to move in and out of their lives as is appropriate for the relationship.

It is impossible for others to reach them beyond surface matters. They are an emotionally closed system and distant in their relationships. It is impossible for them to talk about feelings.

We who come from dysfunctional families and suffer from addictions and codependency know how to sacrifice for others. We know how to give of our time, our money, ourselves, and allow others to walk in and out of our lives at will. If they call us, we'll get the checkbook out, drive the car down, pick them up, and buy them dinner. "What do you need? Watch the kids? OK, I'm there for you." In regard to giving, our boundaries are too permeable.

But we are too shame-bound and closed to receive from others—in that regard, our boundaries are too impermeable. God forbid that we would ever ask for help! We wouldn't dare call someone and tell him that we're in pain, even though everyone in our support group gave us their phone number and insisted we call when in need. "I just couldn't call anybody. They're so busy, and they've got lives. They wouldn't want to hear about me. I couldn't possibly do that."

We keep others out of our lives and harm ourselves in doing so. We also cheat others of serving us in constructive and positive ways.

How have you been violated by boundaries that were too impermeable?

How have you violated another by having boundaries that are too impermeable?

What choices could you make to safeguard against boundaries that are too impermeable?

Based on your answers in this chapter, would you characterize yourself as being primarily a person with boundaries that are too close, too distant, too close and too distant, too rigid, too flexible, too permeable, or too impermeable?

What combination of these make up your personality type?

Write a brief summary of what you learned about yourself as you answered these questions. What thoughts, feelings, and attitudes surfaced or became more clear to you?

Based on what you have learned in this chapter, summarize the new healthy boundaries you can begin to exercise in your relationships.

GROUP EXPERIENCE

Group Leader:

1. Ask if there are any questions about the information in this chapter. Allow others to answer through group discussion.

2. Ask for volunteers who identify with one of the models of unhealthy boundaries in this chapter—one volunteer for each model.

Have them to act out a scenario in which they play the roles of committee members appointed to plan a company picnic. (This is simply a device to give them an opportunity to interact.) Ask each performer to exaggerate acting out his or her part.

Allow them about 15 minutes to interact. When the time is up, ask the performers:

(a) How did you feel playing your role?

(b) Who made you feel most uncomfortable and why?

(c) What feelings were associated with the different roles?

Ask the rest of the group questions b and c.

3. Divide the group into pairs and ask them to share their answers from this chapter that were most significant to them. Also have them tell how they are doing with any new boundaries that they have begun to exercise and evaluate with one another any additional boundaries they have decided to set.

4. Bring the group back together to discuss final questions, thoughts, and feelings.

Set time limits on these group sessions. Remind them that they do not have to share anything they are not ready to share.

– 14 –

Types of People
with Boundary Issues

$\mathcal{P}$eople with boundary issues generally fall into one of the personality types listed below. These are not black and white differences. While we have a tendency to be a combination of all of these types, we will find that one of these are more dominate in us than the others.

We don't become these types overnight. These types develop as a result of the treatment we received as children in our dysfunctional families of origin. We don't all turn out the same even if we came out of the same family. Siblings can have totally different perceptions of what their family was like. When a son talks about Mom and Dad, his brother may wonder, "Did we grow up with the same parents?" Or a sister may ask, "Where was I when all those things you're talking about were going on?"

In their book *Boundaries* Drs. Cloud and Townsend identify types of people who are out of balance and over the line in their boundaries—compliants, avoidants, compliant avoidants, controllers, non-responsives, and controller non-responsives.[1] Be as honest as you can about yourself and identify which of these personality types you are.

COMPLIANTS

Compliants say *yes* to the bad.

Children suffer serious consequences when their parents do not allow them to say *no* when it is right for them to do so. They do not learn how to distinguish the good from the bad and do not even know when bad things are happening to them.

These parents are programming their children to allow others to control, manipulate, and exploit them in adult life. Restricting their *no* handicaps them for life. The children will grow up to be compliant type personalities with boundaries that are too flexible.

We need to be able to say *no* if we are to have a sense of safety. We need to be able to say with confidence, "I disagree." "I will not!" "Stop that!" "It hurts." "It's wrong." "I don't like it when you touch me there!" When we cannot say *no* to the bad, we are automatically saying *yes*.

Here are some of the characteristics of compliants:

Compliants live to meet the needs of others. (This is not the same as meeting the legitimate needs of other persons for whom we have legitimate responsibility, such as that which parents have for their children, and husband and wives have for each other.) We are to take responsibility *for* our own needs and not *for* the needs of others, but we are to be responsive *to* the legitimate needs of others in our relationships. Godly love is doing for others what they cannot do for themselves, expecting nothing in return. Compliants in codependency do for others what those others could and should be doing for themselves and expect a lot in return, yet never allow others to know what those expectations are. The help received from them is the kind of help we'll need help from later on. Codependents rescue people from bearing the consequences of their own behavior.

Compliants enmesh easily with more dominate or opinionated persons.

They tend to like the same things as others do just to get along.

They are like chameleons—changing their behavior, opinions, attitudes, desires, and feelings to conform to those around them.

They take on too many responsibilities and set too few boundaries out of fear of what others might think of them.

They can't say *no* for fear of hurting the other person's feelings.

They fear abandonment and separateness.

They wish to be totally dependent on the other person.

They fear the anger of the other person.

They fear being punished, shamed, and accused of being selfish, bad, or unspiritual.

They fear the overstrict and critical conscience of another person which is experienced as guilt and self-condemnation. Extremely religious people are notorious for self-condemnation because there is a critical parent within them whose judgments add to their impulses to beat up on themselves.

Compliants are very vulnerable to the abuses of controlling, dominating, hidden-agenda spiritual leaders.

Compliants are passive-aggressive. They allow themselves to be used on the outside by the more dominate person, but are resentful of it on the inside. They save their trading stamps and paste them into their little book of resentments until one day they go ballistic and cash them in. "Here's the book with your name on it. I've been waiting for you to say one more thing to me." Afterwards they feel guilty because they exploded and feel that they owe an apology for blowing up. They crawl back into the victim-compliant role and go back to saving up green stamps.

If we are compliant, we need to learn how to think differently about ourselves and how to relate to others. We can feel the pain another person may be having in his life, but we do not have to give him a hundred dollars, move him into our spare bedroom, and take care of him for the next ninety days. We don't have to rescue him from bearing the consequences of his behavior. We can be compassionate on the inside but not give in to his manipulation on the outside.

Do you say *yes* to things you should say *no* to?

Do you allow others to control, manipulate, and exploit you?

Do you live to meet the needs of others?

Do you tend to like the same things as others just to get along?

Do you change your "colors"—attitudes, opinions, and behavior—depending on who you are with?

Do you take on too many responsibilities and set too few boundaries out of fear of what others might think of you?

Are you afraid of hurting other people's feelings if you say *no* to them?

Do you fear abandonment, rejection, and separateness?

Do you wish to be totally dependent on the other person?

Do you fear the anger of the other person?

Do you fear being punished, shamed, and accused of being selfish, bad, or unspiritual?

Do you fear the over-strict and critical conscience of another person?

Do you store up resentments until you explode, then feel guilty for exploding?

If you answered *yes* to three or more of these questions, you are probably an over-the-line compliant type person.

What are some "bads" to which you need to say *no*?

AVOIDANTS

In contrast to compliants, Cloud and Townsend show that avoidants say *no* to the good. They are the children who grow up with boundaries that are rigid and impermeable.

Avoidants are unable to ask for help.

Avoidants usually are unable to recognize their own needs.

If they do recognize their own needs, they set up defenses so that other people who care for them can't get near them to help. They are unable to let others in to help.

They don't want to get involved.

They view their problems as bad, destructive, or shameful. It's OK for other people to have problems, but it is not OK to have problems themselves.

They withdraw and isolate in order to keep others from knowing they have problems. They create a non-human kind of existence.

They put up walls around themselves to keep others out so no one can touch them.

Do you say *no* to things you should say *yes* to?

Is it hard for you to ask for help from others when you really need it?

Do you avoid getting involved with others?

Do you avoid getting involved in events and activities?

Do you have a hard time knowing what your needs really are?

Do you think your problems are bad, destructive, and shameful?

Do you withdraw and isolate from others when you are in need?

Is it hard for you to let others into your life?

If you answered *yes* to three or more of these questions, you are probably an over-the-line avoidant type person.

What are some "good" things to which you need to say *yes*?

COMPLIANT AVOIDANTS

Cloud and Townsend observe that someone can be both a compliant and an avoidant. Compliant avoidants say *yes* to the bad and *no* to the good. These are people who comply to the every wish of others while at the same time are closed to allowing anyone in to help them. Cloud and Townsend say that "compliant avoidants suffer from what is called 'reversed boundaries.'

They have no boundaries where they need them, and they have boundaries where they shouldn't have them." They are people with boundaries that are too flexible on the one hand and too rigid and impermeable on the other hand.

Characteristically, compliant avoidants keep distant the people who are supposed to be close to them, and people who shouldn't be in their lives are throwing up on their living room floor.

They have confused relationships, if any at all; therefore they experience a lot of loneliness and tend to isolate.

They feel empty inside because they are always giving but are unable to receive. They are easily drained and seem to attract user type people into their lives.

Do you often say *yes* to things you should say *no* to and *no* to things you should say *yes* to?

Are you too open to do for others all the time, but unable to allow others to do for you?

Do you have people in your life who shouldn't be there?

Are you confused about your relationships?

Do you keep people at bay who are supposed to be close to you?

Do you experience a lot of loneliness?

Do you tend to isolate from others, especially those who could nurture you?

Do you feel empty and drained because you are always giving but never receiving?

Do you attract people into your life who use you?

Do you experience being too flexible at times only to find out that you brought injury to yourself, then reversed the process and became too rigid?

If you answered *yes* to three or more of these questions, you are probably an over-the-line compliant avoidant type person.

CONTROLLERS

Controllers are identified as another type of person with boundary issues. They are people who have problems respecting the boundaries of others. Cloud and Townsend say, "They resist taking responsibility for their own lives, so they need to control others." They are not able to let others who have poor boundaries take responsibility for their own actions and activities.

They refuse to take *no* for an answer. They know how to say *no,* but don't know how to hear a *no.* Another person's *no* is a controller's challenge to try and change their minds. A *no* means *maybe* and a *maybe* means *yes.*

Controllers don't have ears, figuratively speaking. They cannot hear the needs of other people. They are self-centered and only see their own needs and wants. They are impatient and interruptive. They are those who like to finish your sentences for you.

They cannot accept the needs of others even if they manage to hear what they are. They will try to talk others out of their feelings, opinions, and preferences in order to get them to accept theirs.

They believe it is their job to manage the lives of everyone around them. To be able to control and manage one's life and business in a healthy way is an attribute. But to manipulate others because of a hidden agenda is way out of bounds.

Controllers are good at shifting responsibility for their own lives onto others. They will come up with all kinds of good ideas for others to carry out. They need those other people to perform their good ideas for them in order to make them look good. But they are usually unable to carry through on their own ideas. They have to resort to manipulating others to get these ideas in operation. However, most people are not able to live up to the expectations of a controller which sets the controller up for resentment.

Cloud and Townsend make a distinction between aggressive controllers and manipulative controllers. The aggressive controller lives in a world of *yes.* They are out front with their control issues. They don't pay attention to the boundaries of others because they don't realize that other people have boundaries or have a right to them. They can be very verbally and physically abusive persons.

Manipulative controllers, on the other hand, are less direct than aggressive controllers. They are more argumentative than commanding and try to con people out of their boundaries.

Cloud and Townsend say, "They indirectly manipulate circumstances to get their way. They seduce others into carrying their burdens. They use guilt messages." Yet, they "deny their desires to control others."

"I'm not controlling, what are you talking about? I'm just trying to tell you that if you would do certain things, I'd be able to get along with you better and we wouldn't be having all of these problems."

"Compliant avoidants," says Cloud and Townsend, "can also be manipulative controllers." They have hidden agendas for why they do what they do for others. You have to be a mind reader to live with a manipulative controller. They give in order to get. So, their caring for the other person ends up being an indirect means of controlling that other person. "I love you. How can you treat me this way?" They will guilt-provoke the other person into loving them back.

The book *Alcoholics Anonymous* talks about control and manipulation. It says that an alcoholic may be a compliant, nurturing, caring, supportive person one minute, but, when that doesn't get the response he wants, the next minute he becomes a belligerent, aggressive, dominating, loud person.

Controllers have rigid rules of self-control. They set up rigid control vows and do not allow themselves to violate them. "I'm always in control. I never lose control." A person goes to therapy with guarded comments, "I don't know if I want to continue doing this."

"Why?" the therapist asks.

"I'm afraid I'll lose it."

"What happens if you lose it?"

"I may not get it back. I may end up being that guy in the nut-house who's gone and will never come back."

Controllers not only try to control others but are very controlled themselves. They are so controlled that they are often out of control. Their control issues wreak havoc all around them.

True active controllers will not be able to answer the following questions. They are unable to see that they are controlling and have no respect for other people's boundaries. You must be willing to take a hard and honest look at yourself to answer the following questions.

Do you have problems respecting other people's boundaries?

Do you resist taking responsibility for your own life and business?

Do you try to control and manipulate other people's lives and business?

Do you refuse to take *no* for an answer?

Do you finish other people's sentences and thoughts for them?

Do you try to talk people out of their feelings, opinions, and preferences?

Aggressive controller

Are you verbally abusive?

Are you physically abusive?

Manipulative controller

Are you argumentative?

Do you try to con or guilt-provoke other people into doing or not doing things to suit you?

Do you do for others so they will do for you?

Do you think people ought to know about your needs without your having to tell them what they are?

Do you have rigid rules of self-control?

Do other people say any of the above things about you?

If you answered *yes* to three or more of these questions, you are probably an over-the-line controller type person.

If you answered *yes* to either of the two questions under aggressive controller, you are one. If you answered *yes* to two or more of the questions under manipulative controller, you are one. If you answered in both, you are most likely both.

What measures can you take to be less controlling?

NON-RESPONSIVES

Another type of person with boundary problems, according to Cloud and Townsend, are non-responsives. They are people who are unable to connect to the needs and feelings of others.

Non-responsives neglect their responsibilities in relationships which blocks the possibility of achieving intimacy. They set boundaries against the responsibility to love. The wife complains, "I just want him to talk to me." The male in a marital counseling situation is usually a non-responsive, compliant-avoidant. He cannot respond to the emotional needs of his wife and says *yes* when he doesn't mean it.

Though we are not responsible *for* our spouses' emotional well-being, we should be responsive *to* them. We need to hear our spouses' emotional needs and meet them as we can. The person who is with a non-responsive is constantly trying to get him or her to respond. However, it is not our job to teach our mates how to open up emotionally. The more we try to get non-responsives to respond, the further they move away from us. It is our job to be who we are and set our boundaries.

Non-responsives may be grouped into two categories: critical and narcissistic.

Critical non-responsives are those who are critical toward the needs of others and hate the fact that they have needs of their own. This ties back to the avoidant who feels he doesn't deserve to have needs, and he doesn't think others should have needs either.

150

Narcissistic non-responsives are "those who are so absorbed in their own desires and needs that they exclude others." Narcissism results when one did not get his narcissistic needs meet during his developmental stages.

Is it difficult for you to connect to the needs and feelings of others?

Is it hard for you to reach out with love for others, including the closest members of your family?

Are you critical toward the needs of others?

Are you absorbed in your own desires and needs to the point that you don't have room in your life for others?

If you answered *yes* to three or more of these questions, you are probably an over-the-line non-responsive type person.

What measures can you take to be more responsive?

CONTROLLER NON-RESPONSIVES

Finally, Cloud and Townsend identify the controlling non-responsive as a type of person with boundary problems. They are self-absorbed people who are looking for someone else to take care of them. "They gravitate toward someone with blurry boundaries, who will naturally take on too many responsibilities in the relationship and who won't complain about it."

Controlling non-responsives come into your life, hating their own needs. They have needs but are never going to tell you about them. They want you to read their minds and take care of them. If you don't do it right, they're going to manipulatively control you to get it done. You're not supposed to have needs, and, if you do, they'll squelch them and press in harder for you to take care of them. They will find a compliant avoidant to hook up with.

Do you look to other people to take care of you and your problems who won't complain?

Do you hate it that you have so many problems?

Do you hide your needs from others?

Do you get angry inside of yourself when people don't take care of your business for you as you think they should?

Do you then manipulate them even harder to take care of you?

If you answered *yes* to three or more of these questions, you are probably an over-the-line avoidant type person.

What measures can you take to be less of a controller non-responsive?

Two final questions: Where did you find the person that you invited into your life to violate your boundaries?

What drew you to this person?

These personality types reveal themselves when we enter into intimate relationships. If we are not presently in a relationship, those strongest tendencies are probably not activated. But get into a relationship and within no time at all our dominate thought disorders will surface.

Based on your answers in this chapter, would you characterize yourself as being primarily a compliant, avoidant, compliant/avoidant, controller, non-responsive, controller/non-responsive?

Do you see yourself as a combination of these types? Describe.

Based on what you have learned in this chapter, summarize the new healthy boundaries you can begin to exercise in your relationships.

GROUP EXPERIENCE

Group Leader:
1. Ask if there are any questions about the information in this chapter. Allow others to answer through group discussion.

2. Ask the group to think of someone who is a compliant type person.
Ask a volunteer to give this person a fictitious name and tell a story about this person that best depicts them as a compliant.
Repeat this activity for an avoidant, a compliant-avoidant, a controller, a non-responsive, and a controller non-responsive. Make sure everyone understands these distinctions.

3. Divide the group into pairs and ask them to share their answers from this chapter that were most significant to them. Also have them tell how they are doing with any new boundaries that they have begun to exercise and evaluate with one another any additional boundaries they have decided to set.

4. Bring the group back together to discuss final questions, thoughts, and feelings.

Set time limits on these group sessions. Remind them that they do not have to share anything they are not ready to share.

— 15 —

Resolving the Losses

We have discovered by now that we were raised in a family that was dysfunctional, we have suffered some abuse to one degree or another, and we have some boundary problems. All of this has a lot to do with who we are and with the problems we may be having in relationships.

Now we want to show how the abuses we have suffered have resulted in losses in our lives. These losses have caused us to behave in ways that we think will keep us safe from further loss. Resolving these losses is the key to being able to set and maintain healthy boundaries.

It is time to assess these losses, position ourselves to be healed from the damage that these losses have caused, and begin to strengthen our boundaries for a more peaceful and successful life.

As you work through this chapter, you will be asked to make note of major events of loss in your life. A form is provided at the end of this chapter to assist you in doing so. You will then be challenged to identify the losses that are associated with each of these events, determine how you have compensated for those losses, determine where you are in the grieving process, ask God for healing and strength, and set goals to take back those losses that are retrievable.

Loss events

Loss events occur when something happens that takes something from us. These events may be due to natural causes or due to abuse in our lives. In either case we usually feel violated and angry. Losses occur in all of the five life areas we have covered in this workbook: relational, spiritual, physical, sexual, and emotional.

Relational losses occur because of deaths, divorces, abandonment, disagreements, separations, drug and alcohol use, incarcerations—anything that disrupts our connectedness and interdependence with other persons, animals, and things. For example: I lost my dad when he left home. I lost my dog when he got run over by a car. I lost my best friend when his family moved across country. I lost my brother when he started using drugs.

Spiritual losses occur with all abuses. If the spiritual leader in our lives fails to provide spiritual nurturing, if the teachings upon which we build our lives prove to be invalid, if addictions and compulsive behaviors rob us of our power, then these boundary violations hinder our relationship with God and we incur losses in the area of spirituality. Anything that prohibits us from being aware of and responsive to God has the potential to set us up for primary and secondary losses.

Physical losses occur with health problems, dismemberment, bankruptcy, natural disasters, fire, theft—anything that robs us of natural and physical well-being and property. For example: I lost my health to a major heart attack. I lost my leg in a motorcycle wreck. I lost my house and automobiles when I lost my job. I lost my irreplaceable valuables when our house burned down.

Sexual losses occur with abusive sexual violations, shaming sexual comments to us as children, absence of a parent, surgery, aging—anything that threatens our wholeness as a sexual being. For example: I lost my virginity when I was sexually violated as a child. I lost my sexual identity growing up without a dad in my life.

Emotional losses occur through abuses of all kinds, improper mirroring of emotions during our formative years, being made to feel ashamed for having feelings, traumatic experiences that cause us to shut down—anything that causes us to be out of touch with our true emotions. For example: I lost my childhood because I had to be my mother's best friend and surrogate spouse.

List the losses you have experienced relationally.

List the losses you have experienced spiritually.

List the losses you have experienced physically.

List the losses you have experienced sexually.

List the losses you have experienced emotionally.

Using the form on pages 162-164, write a brief description of your loss events as you have identified them in this workbook. By rewriting them, you may uncover new insights. To do this, answer items 1 and 2 on the form.

Existential losses

David Damico in his book *Faces of Rage* has identified eight losses that hide behind the more obvious losses that we experience.[1] These losses touch us at a far deeper and more meaningful level of our existence. These *existential* losses are the real losses and are to be distinguished from the loss events listed above.

What we have really lost, he says, is safety, purpose, significance, authenticity, eligibility, hope, dignity, and power. These losses are not automatically resolved with the passage of time.

Safety is a natural, universal, and legitimate need. If we were abused growing up, we experienced abandonment and that abandonment left us feeling unsafe. When our safety is threatened, we "typically respond with fear, anger, or both."

Likewise, we all need to feel like our lives have some *purpose* to them. This sense of purpose for our lives is taken from us "when our attempts to contribute are rejected, scorned, criticized, stolen, or ignored."

In a similar way, our feelings of *significance* are taken from us when our achievements are not recognized and appreciated.

Authenticity means that we are different from each other. We need to be able to recognize and appreciate our own differences and have those differences recognized and appreciated by others. But, if we were not allowed to be different, unique, or special, then we had to adopt false selves in order to survive. Conformity is the guiding rule in all of our institutions—home, church, and school. We walk in as individuals and march out as clones of that institution. We have to adapt to the expectations of others who want us to be what they want us to be rather than allowing us to emerge into the unique persons we potentially are.

We experience the loss of *eligibility* when others reject us, show prejudice against us, or make unfair judgments against us. Abusive statements that are made to us make us feel disqualified to enter into relationships. "An individual who struggles with the loss of eligibility," writes Damico, "has a profound sense of inadequacy and self-hate."

If we suffer too many losses in our lives, we will lose *hope*. "Hope helps us endure crises....Hopelessness usually comes when we find ourselves in crisis and we can see no end, can find no friend, can exercise no options, can experience no rest." We compensate with fantasies of false hope which only set us up for greater disappointments and losses.

The loss of safety, purpose, authenticity, eligibility, and hope diminishes our self-respect and acceptance. We therefore suffer the loss of *dignity*. We are often put in embarrassing, shaming, humiliating situations as children of dysfunction and abuse.

Finally, we suffer the loss of *power*. "Abuse in all its forms is disempowering." Power is that energy that motivates us to live active, vibrant lives. Damico writes, "Power is the ability to reach out, explore, choose, interpret, risk, challenge, and perceive."

Using the form on pages 162-164, identify the existential losses you have suffered that apply to the event you are processing. To do this, answer item 3 on the form.

Primary and Secondary Losses

Damico also talks about primary and secondary losses.[2] The initial event that brings about a primary loss in our lives may be the result of circumstances, irresponsible parenting, an act of lawless disobedience, societal prejudice, upheaval, chaos, or generational sin. In a nurturing context, losses are recognized and resolved constructively. When the primary loss is not resolved, it sets a pattern for secondary losses to occur. We don't know how to resolve them, and so they build upon each other.

Damico gives the example of ten-year-old Jimmy who lost his dad to death. This was the first loss event and it triggered physical and emotional abandonment for Jimmy. Jimmy's existential losses were hope, safety, and power. These losses were not resolved, so he became predisposed to secondary losses. His mother remarried years later and Jimmy's hope for a dad were smashed when his step-dad mistreated him and showed special preference to his own children. Once again Jimmy experienced physical and emotional abandonment with the added element of abuse. His existential losses were dignity, significance, and authenticity. "The secondary losses that Jimmy suffered were more wounding because they reinforced his feelings of powerlessness, hopelessness, and fear."

Using the form on pages 162-164, write about how an unresolved primary loss has left you open to subsequent losses that you have not been able to resolve. To do this, answer item 4 on the form.

Compensating for the losses

Unresolved losses create feelings of rage within us. Damico defines rage as "a self-protective shield we use to avoid loss-threatening circumstances or events." It is the only emotion strong enough to insulate us from the pain of these losses.[3] Yet, we hide the rage behind a variety of self-defeating behaviors that share a common motive—the need for control. Thus we make for ourselves "performance vows" or "control vows" in an attempt to prevent future loss.[4]

Performance vows address *methods* of behavior. They tell us how we are supposed to act to keep our world running the way we think it is supposed to run. These vows produce in us a perfectionist, cynical, sarcastic, activist, and legalistic type personality. We have no room for making mistakes, therefore we limit ourselves to what we know we can succeed at doing. We adopt performance vows to try to correct the behavior that allowed us to be susceptible to the abuse and loss.

Control vows, on the other hand, address *rules* for behavior. "Control vows are made when someone breaks the rules and, in doing so, exposes us to loss," writes Damico.

These vows are damaging and need to be broken because they are not real solutions. They are the smoke screens for rage and unresolved losses.

There are two kinds of control: inward (covert) and outward (overt). Most of us have a combination of both, but one or the other will be our preference.

Inward control is a sense or feeling of always having to be in control of ourselves inwardly. We would never allow ourselves to lose it: to laugh uncontrollably, play, show anger, etc. We wouldn't let anyone know how disturbed we were about a situation. We would flex our inward emotional muscles through whatever face of rage we are using to stay in control. Chronic inward control is the root of phobic behavior. Agoraphobiacs don't want to leave their houses because they can't control things out in public. What goes on out there makes them have anxiety attacks. Since they can't control what is going on outside of themselves, they become more obsessed trying to control what is going on inside. The more they try to control themselves within, the more they cut themselves off from the outside. This creates more fear and more rage.

Outward control is more obvious to others. We try to tell others how to live their lives, boss others around, and generally try to take control of every situation.

Inward control is not as obvious, but is more manipulative. If I am staying in control in here and I won't let anything out, you don't know what I am feeling or thinking which has a tendency to force you into "mind reading"—a well known characteristic of dysfunctional families. This is another form of manipulation. We will use manipulation to get what we want.

Though we speak of performance and control vows separately, in real life we usually combine these vows. Note how you combine these vows as they relate to your loss events.

Using the form on pages 162-164, identify the performance and/or control vows you have made to avoid future loss-threatening circumstances or events associated with each loss event. To do this answer item 5 on the form, for example:

Grieving the losses

Some of the losses in our lives may be retrievable, but most are not. We need to examine each loss realistically and grieve those that are irretrievable so we can get past them and be healed from them. The grief process has been documented by Elisabeth Kubler-Ross in her book *On Death and Dying*: it goes from denial to anger, bargaining, depression, and ultimately to acceptance.[5] These grief stages apply with any kind of loss. We are not consciously aware that we are going through these stages. We may skip some stages, revert back to a former stage, or get stuck in a stage. Our understanding of this process helps us to deal with the losses associated with abuse.

Stage One - Denial. It is our tendency to overlook things that are painful. "This is not happening to me." "There's no problem here." If someone else suggests that there is a problem, we rationalize it by saying, "It's just a phase," or we minimize it by saying, "It isn't too bad." A realistic look at the loss is essential to go beyond this stage.

Stage Two - Anger. Once we come out of denial and face the reality of the loss, we discover that we are angry about it. "Why did they do this to me?" or "I don't deserve this," are examples of something we might say to ourselves. The abuse has made us feel shameful and inadequate which means that we may be just as angry at ourselves as we are toward the other person. Anger tells us that an abuse has taken place. It is OK to have anger and to find healthy ways to express it. Suppressing it *never* disarms it. As long as we deny that we are angry, we will be stuck in it. Sooner or later, we have to realize that suppressed anger does little good for either party.

Stage Three - Bargaining. Once we come out of denial and experience anger, we realize that we are not in control. This frightens us. When we cannot control what is happening to us, we will try to bargain with our offender. We will try to salvage anything we can among the losses. Bargaining is usually unsuccessful and may lead back to anger or onward to depression. Bargaining is another method of attempting control. We must realize that we do not have the power or the responsibility to control another person's choice. This realization may result in a feeling of helplessness and depression.

Stage Four - Depression. Depression occurs when we have tried everything and nothing has worked. Our anger is turned inward. We have lost all control. An overwhelming sense of guilt and shame are felt. At this point, we usually need therapy, a group, and a sovereign act of God to help us move on to the final stage of grieving.

Stage Five - Acceptance. The only resolution for grief is acceptance. Acceptance is not adopting a fatalistic attitude in order to cope, but is the funeral service that puts finality on the loss and releases us from the grief.
A recovering alcoholic once wrote:

> And acceptance is the answer to *all* my problems today. When I am disturbed, it is because I find some person, place, thing, or situation—some fact of my life—unacceptable to me, and I can find no serenity until I accept that person, place, thing, or situation as being exactly the way it is supposed to be at this moment. Nothing, absolutely nothing happens in God's world by mistake. Until I could accept my alcoholism, I could not stay sober; unless I accept life completely on life's terms, I cannot be happy. I need to concentrate not so much on what needs to be changed in the world as on what needs to be changed in me and in my attitudes.[6]

At this point, you need to find out where you are in the grief process. The moment that you identify where you are and own that, you will immediately begin to move to other stages. Be prepared to experience the anger, bargaining, and depression that is already hidden in you. Knowing where you are in the grief process gives hope that you can move along and resolve the losses.

Using the form on pages 162-164, answer where you are in the grieving process. To do this, answer item 6 on the form.

Setting goals to take back the losses

Some losses are retrievable. We can choose to restore them if we like. Goal setting is a good discipline to help us achieve our dreams and restore those losses. When something comes along that does not fit in with our goals, we can establish a boundary and say *no* to it. We take back control of our lives. We recommend the goal setting section found in Step Ten of the *Power to Choose: Twelve Steps to Wholeness* book/workbook. It will guide you in a thorough goal-setting process.[7]

Goal setting is a process that provides the motivation for us to:
- set healthy boundaries and restore the losses,
- have a life that we've never had before,
- stop allowing others to violate us, and
- stop violating the boundaries of other people.

Using the form on pages 162-164, evaluate the realistic possibility of your loss being restored and state the goals you intend to work toward to restore that loss. To do this, answer item 7 on the form.

Ultimately, we need to be healed from the emotional damage we have suffered from these losses. Hopefully that healing has begun in the process of doing this work. Ultimately we will find that our purpose, significance, authenticity, eligibility, hope, dignity, and power are in God and not in people and things that will ultimately fail us because of their own powerlessness.

WORKING THROUGH THE LOSSES

Using the following format, write about each loss-producing event. Start with the earliest event that you can remember, then write about subsequent events in chronological order.

A special notebook may be helpful for this purpose and will allow for processing future losses as they may occur. Take note of the chart on page 164 as an additional aid.

Refer to the text as needed to make sure you understand the meaning of terms used here.

1. Write the age span during which the event took place: 0-6, 7-12, 13-18, etc., up to your present age.

2. Briefly describe the event:

3. Which of these eight existential losses did you experience because of the event? (Circle the ones that apply).

Safety   Purpose   Significance   Authenticity   Eligibility   Hope   Dignity   Power

4. What subsequent losses have you been exposed to that you have not been able to resolve as the result of this primary loss in your life?

5. What performance vow have you made to compensate for the losses relating to the event?

What control vow have you made to compensate for the losses relating to the event?

6. Check where you are in the grieving process for each existential loss.

	Denial	Anger	Bargaining	Depression	Acceptance
Safety					
Purpose					

	Denial	Anger	Bargaining	Depression	Acceptance
Significance					
Authenticity					
Eligibility					
Hope					
Dignity					
Power					

Complete the following sentence:
      In order to grieve this loss I need to

7. Some of these losses must be accepted as lost forever, but some can be restored. Evaluate which applies to this event. If the losses can be restored, what realistic goals can be set for achieving that restoration? Complete the following questions:

What new relational goals do you need to set for restoring loss?

What new spiritual goals do you need to set for restoring loss?

What new physical goals do you need to set for restoring loss?

What new sexual goals do you need to set for restoring loss?

What new emotional goals do you need to set for restoring loss?

What other goals do you need to set for restoring loss?

Chart

You may want to make your own form like the one below to chart your losses and note your vows as you fill in items 1, 2, 3, and 5 of the worksheet. The examples given may help you to formulate your answers.

Age span	Event	LOSSES								Performance Vow	Control Vow
		Safety	Purpose	Significance	Authenticity	Eligibility	Hope	Dignity	Power		
	RELATIONAL										
0-6 7-12	Father physically gone, working two jobs	x		x		x				Perform perfectly for acceptance	Never get close to a man
	SPIRITUAL										
0-6 7-12	Lack of intimacy with Dad—transferred to God	x		x	x	x		x	x	Perform for acceptance by church	Don't let anyone know who I really am
	PHYSICAL										
0-9	Never had my own space growing up	x		x	x				x	Perform for acceptance and to feel significant	Have my own area and not share it with anyone
	SEXUAL										
12-18	Inappropriate touching from uncle	x	x	x	x	x	x	x	x	I'll always be in charge of sexual activity	No man will ever use me for sex
	EMOTIONAL										
0-18	Both parents were emotionally distant	x		x			x	x		Take care of myself in all areas always	Don't ever admit to having needs

GROUP EXPERIENCE

Group Leader:
1. Ask if there are any questions about the information in this chapter. Allow others to answer through group discussion.

2. Ask the group to give examples of existential losses and discuss them.

3. Divide the group into pairs and ask them to share their answers from this chapter that were most significant to them. Also have them tell how they are doing with any new boundaries that they have begun to exercise and evaluate with one another any additional boundaries they have decided to set.

4. Bring the group back together to discuss final questions, thoughts, and feelings.

5. Remind the group that the next session will be the last one unless an extension has been planned.

Set time limits on these group sessions. Remind them that they do not have to share anything they are not ready to share.

– 16 –

Forgiveness

People sometimes do mean things to us on purpose. Sometimes we do mean things to others on purpose. But most of the time we just do things and those things bring injury to others. These injurious things we do to others, whether intentional or not, are boundary violations. When a boundary has been violated, certain corrections have to be made. We not only need to establish strong and healthy boundaries where they did not previously exist, but we must find a way to forgive the offenders of the past. Forgiveness is the resolution of unforgiveness. It is necessary in order for us to heal from the hurt, the resentments, and the bitterness.

FORGIVENESS IS NOT AN EMOTION

It feels good to forgive and to be forgiven, but there is more to forgiveness than feelings. "Feeling" forgiveness toward someone in any given moment doesn't mean we have forgiven that person. It only means we are having some warm fuzzies in that moment. If we have not truly forgiven someone, those resentments will find cause to show their angry faces again.

Resentments, whether we are conscious of them or not, are usually associated with the loss events in our lives. We resent a person or a group of persons who are sometimes hidden behind systems and institutions and unfair laws, rules, and regulations. When those resentments are present, we find ourselves periodically, if not all of the time, carrying on mental arguments (ruminations of the mind) with these people. This is a sure sign that we hold a resentment toward them. We all do this, so there is no need to feel ashamed about it. Nevertheless, we can be set free from these ruminations (also called "rehearsings") if we deal with them appropriately.

What thoughts (ruminations) still run through your mind that have to do with the loss events in your life? Be sure to review each event.

What resentments are you feeling? Answer by completing these sentences:

"I resent _____ for _____!"

"I resent _____ for _____!"

"I resent _____ for _____!"

"I resent _____ for _____!"

"I resent _____ for _____!"

Some of us want to keep our resentments. We think that we are getting even with the offender as long as we carry the grudge. But nothing ever really gets evened up. Unforgiveness not only gives the offender more power in our lives, but it holds us hostage to our own bad feelings.

SOME QUALITIES OF FORGIVENESS

Forgiveness frees us to be at peace with the offender without having to continue to receive the offense.

We mistakenly think that if we forgive an abusive person we have to stay in an abusive relationship with that person. This is not so. We need to forgive others who have offended us in order for us to get at peace with ourselves, but we do not have to continue the patterns of abuse in our lives. That is why we need to set new boundaries at the same time we try to forgive.

Forgiving offenders does not mean that they cannot be punished for their crimes. They must face the consequences of their actions. That's between them, God, and the law.

Forgiveness helps us to set boundaries against resentment.

Resentment and unforgiveness are violations against our own emotional well-being. Forgiveness is the antidote to resentment and unforgiveness. It teaches us how to handle our feelings in the face of future boundary violations and protects us from further resentments and unforgivenesses which threaten our emotional well-being. Forgiveness is like a boundary in itself. I have a boundary that will not allow your treatment of me to cause further resentment in me.

Forgiveness helps to move us past hurtful events in our lives.

Unforgiveness and resentment can kill us if we hold on to them. We can't keep our resentments and recover from the pain of the boundary violations at the same time.

FORGIVING OTHERS

Resentment means we want something from the offender. He or she owes us a debt. A dictionary meaning of forgiveness is "to excuse for a fault or an offense; pardon; to renounce anger or resentment against; to absolve from payment of (a debt, for example)."[1] So forgiveness is releasing someone from a debt.

When we have a resentment toward another, we need to decide what we think that person owes us. He may owe us money, an apology, a favor, or something else. We, then, need to write it down on paper, take a good look at it, and decide if we want to forgive him of that debt.

It is not easy to forgive our offenders. We may not "feel" like doing it. Nevertheless, it is better to verbalize the forgiveness and get it out into the open than to retain it.

Begin by faithfully completing the following "you owe me" statements. This is your "debtors list."

Name the persons you resent and write what you think they owe you.

(Name of the offender) _____ , you owe me _____
_____because you _____
_____.

(Name of the offender) _____ , you owe me _____
_____because you _____
_____.

(Name of the offender) _____ , you owe me _____
_____because you _____
_____.

(Name of the offender) _____ , you owe me _____
_____because you _____
_____.

(Name of the offender) _____ , you owe me _____
_____because you _____
_____.

Those debts that we think people owe us fall into two categories: those that can realistically be collected and those that cannot. If they can be collected, we need to list that option. If they cannot be collected, we need to accept the losses created by the debts. We need to discern the difference between what is collectible and what is not.

A collectible debt is one that can be paid. The debtor may not pay it, but it could realistically be paid.

For example, Butch owes Marty $250. Marty calls Butch and asks, "What are you going to do about that?" Butch may respond, (1) "I'll put a check in the mail today," (2) "I don't have $250, but I'll make a regular payment every week until it's all paid," or (3) "I didn't borrow that money. You gave it to me. I ain't gonna pay." If Marty gets answer number three, he can hound Butch, sue him, or accept his answer and forgive (release) the debt.

A non-collectible debt is another matter. Marty's dad died when he was six years old. He not only lost his dad, but lost a part of his childhood. He feels that his dad not only owes him a dad, but a childhood. He cannot bring Dad back to pay the debt, so he has to look to other options. Examples are: (1) seek out another man to represent Dad in order to restore the losses, (2) grieve the losses and come to acceptance, (3) self-nurture the child within by buying the electric train he always wanted but never had, or (4) look to God as Father.

Write down the debts on your debtors list that are realistic, tangible, and collectible; and list the available options that will be acceptable to you.

Now that you have completed your lists, set an empty chair in front of you and pretend those offenders, one at a time, are sitting in that chair. Go back over your debtors list, and read the items aloud that pertain to the offender as if you were speaking directly to that person. Be sure to name all of the offenses you can possibly think of.

(Name of the offender) _____, I forgive you for (name the offense)_____.

(Name of the offender) _____, I forgive you for (name the offense)_____.

(Name of the offender) _____, I forgive you for (name the offense)_____.

(Name of the offender) _____, I forgive you for (name the offense)_____.

(Name of the offender) _____, I forgive you for (name the offense)_____.

Now write the names of the people you honestly feel you have forgiven and, therefore, do not owe you a debt any longer.

If we are the offenders, we need to ask forgiveness when possible and make amends as needed. Complete these sentences:

I offended _____ when I _____

_____
and I need to ask forgiveness.

I offended _____ when I _____

_____
and I need to ask forgiveness.

I offended _____ when I _____

_____
and I need to ask forgiveness.

I offended _____ when I _____

_____
and I need to ask forgiveness.

I offended _____ when I _____

_____
and I need to ask forgiveness.

FORGIVING OURSELVES

If we have been violated and feel that the offender owes us something, we are likely to feel obligated to hold on to resentment or the need for revenge. We take on a debt ourselves—"I'm gonna pay him back for that!" We feel that we will betray ourselves if we don't keep our vow or if we give up our resentment. We want what the Old Testament calls "an eye for an eye." But we need to resolve these vengeful feelings in our hearts and let the legal system (or God) take care of the punishments. We need to forgive ourselves of this debt.

The following statements are to help us forgive ourselves of the vengeful vows we feel indebted to keep. Make note of how you devised to "pay them back."

Complete the "pay them back" statements as needed.

I now release myself from the vow to pay _____ back for

by _____ .

I now release myself from the vow to pay _____ back for

by _____ .

I now release myself from the vow to pay _____ back for

by _____ .

I now release myself from the vow to pay _____ back for

by _____ .

I now release myself from the vow to pay _____ back for

by _____ .

Also, we have done things to others for which we are remorseful. We may not be forgiven by them, but we can and must forgive ourselves with the resolve to "go and sin no more."

I now forgive myself for _____

_____ .

I now forgive myself for _____

_____ .

I now forgive myself for _____

_____ .

I now forgive myself for _____

_____ .

I now forgive myself for _____

_____ .

FORGIVING GOD

We frequently blame God for the things that happen to us whether or not God really had anything to do with the loss. Our feelings have no regard for religion and theology. If we have anger and resentment toward God, we are perceiving that he had something to do with it. If the anger and resentment is there, we need to find it in our hearts to forgive God the same way we have just forgiven others and ourselves.

How have you blamed God for what has happened to you?

What do you think God owes you?

Are you willing to forgive God for what you perceive he has done or allowed to be done to you?

POWERLESSNESS

Even if we don't want to hang on to our resentments, we often find that we are still powerless to forgive. We have to take the first step of becoming willing to forgive. Forgiveness doesn't come from self-effort. It comes from letting God's mercy flow into our hearts. It has to be his forgiveness working through our hearts.

Before we can even become willing to forgive, we have to get honest and admit to God, "I don't forgive these people. I've been lying. I've been praying for them everyday for a year, but I haven't forgiven them anything. That's the truth, God. So, I'm powerless to forgive these people. That's some bad news. Some worse news, God, is that I've just found out that you love them just as much as you love me. I'm really bummed out about that. I want mercy and forgiveness for me, but I want justice for them! And I have the whole justice plan laid out here for them—exactly how they are to repay me for what they have done to me."

Powerlessness means that we are powerless to forgive in and of ourselves, and we have to have God's power, mercy, and grace to come into our hearts to give us this ability—his power, mercy, and grace not ours, because we don't have power, mercy, and grace. We have an "eye for an eye."

What resentments do you want to give up but have been powerless to do so?

What feelings are you still left with?

Are you willing to give those feelings to God and have him remove them?

You may not yet "feel" any better about forgiving the offender(s) in your life, but can you imagine how it would feel to be released from all of that hurt and bitterness? Take a moment and try to imagine it.

Group Experience

Group Leader:

1. Ask if there are any questions about the information in this chapter. Allow others to answer through group discussion.

2. This is the final group experience called for in this workbook. If this is your last group meeting as well, be sure to provide proper closure.

(a) Ask for brief testimonies on how group members experienced forgiveness.

(b) Ask for brief testimonies on how lives have been changed in the process of going through this workbook.

(c) Ask if there are thoughts, feelings, questions, or problems yet unresolved.

(d) Read the elements of Chapter 18 on maintenance.

(e) Find out if there is a desire among the members to continue a support group. If so, let them decide whether to continue on as they are, or whether to form new groups for themselves.

3. Optional: Divide the group into pairs and ask them to share the most meaningful response that they wrote for the questions in this chapter.

4. Ask the group to discuss final questions, thoughts, and feelings.

5. Write and tell us about your experiences—successes, problems, innovations.

c/o Power Life Resources
237 Nunley Drive
Nashville, TN 37211

Set a time limit on these group session. Remind them that they do not have to share anything they are not ready to share.

– 17 –

Maintenance

Our unhealthy boundaries are the result of a lifetime of being involved in unhealthy, dysfunctional systems. Redefining ourselves and establishing healthy boundaries are not simple matters. We have to unlearn the old and establish the new. Although it takes time, new and healthy boundaries can be established and strengthened with practice.

Our boundaries need to be clear, uncomplicated, unapologetic, and sure. We have to pay constant attention to them. They do not suddenly become a part of our lives with the wave of a magic wand.

Here are some follow-up steps you should consider taking to maintain strong boundaries.

GET IN A SUPPORT GROUP

Getting in a support group is of absolute necessity. We need relationships who will support us as we go through these changes in our lives. Unhealthy relationships have been the problem, so it will take being in healthy relationships to help heal the problem.

Being in a small, confidential support group can provide a safe place for us
- to talk about healthy boundaries,
- to learn about them,
- to practice and strengthen them,
- to get feedback about ourselves and our feelings, and

• to have accountability as we walk out healthy boundaries in our relationships. We need others who will tell us the truth about what they see happening in our lives.

ACCEPT RESPONSIBILITY

In the past we have had the tendency to shift the blame for our troubles on others. If we were abused, it seems obvious that the abuses were the fault of other people. And indeed they were the perpetrators of the abuse. But we can no longer remain passive to and accepting of their abuses. We teach others how to treat us. In many cases, the abuse that we have received from others is the result of poor boundaries on our part.

Now we have the opportunity to accept responsibility for what we allow others to do to us, and we can do something about that. We have the power to say *no*.

We need to accept responsibility for our violations against others as well.

WORK THE TWELVE STEPS

In addition to completing this workbook, we strongly recommend that you form a support group of two to six persons of your same sex and work through the Twelve Steps as presented in the *Power to Choose: Twelve Steps to Wholeness* book/workbook. This process enables you to make peace with God, make peace with yourself, and make peace with others. In so doing, it will also strengthen your ability to set and maintain healthy boundaries.

KEEP A DAILY JOURNAL

Keep a journal of daily experiences:

Describe incidents in which you stood strongly in your boundaries, incidents in which boundary violations were avoided, and incidents in which boundary violations occurred. Think about how you let people treat you, talk with you, and interact with you.

Describe your feelings about what happened. Were you OK with that?

Describe the messages that boundary violations sent to your body, emotions, and/or spirit.

State what boundary you lacked or what boundary helped you. What personal values did you discount or hold on to?

Describe how you were responsible for a violation occurring or being avoided.

Suggest how you can better handle similar experiences in the future.

GET PROFESSIONAL HELP IF NEEDED

Some people may find that working on boundary issues is extremely painful. Some may find that their issues go beyond the intent or scope of this workbook. If this is true of you, we urge you to seek professional help to guide you through this recovery process.

Source Notes

Chapter 2   What Are Boundaries?

1. Anne Katherine, *Boundaries: Where You End and I Begin* (Park Ridge, IL: Parkside Publishing, 1991), p. 3. © 1991 Hazelden Foundation, Center City, Minnesota.
2. Drs. Henry Cloud and John Townsend, *Boundaries: When to Say YES, When to Say NO, To Take Control of Your Life* (Grand Rapids, MI: Zondervan, 1992), p. 29.
3. Ibid., p. 151.

Chapter 3   Why Boundaries?

1. Katherine, *Boundaries*, p. 39.

Chapter 4   Characteristics of Persons with Healthy Boundaries

1. Katherine, *Boundaries*, p. 81.

Chapter 5   Where We Learn Boundaries

1. Cloud and Townsend, *Boundaries*, pp. 171-172.
2. Ibid., pp. 72-73.
3. These roles were first described by Sharon Wegscheider-Cruse in *The Family Trap*, (Minneapolis: Johnson Institute, 1976).
4. Melody Beattie, *Codependent No More* (New York: Harper & Row, 1987), p. 31.
5. Mike S. O'Neil and Charles E. Newbold, *The Church As a Healing Community* (Nashville, TN: Sonlight Publishing, 1995).

Chapter 8   Relational Boundaries

1. *Alcoholics Anonymous*, 3d ed., (New York: Alcoholics Anonymous World Services, Inc., 1976). The Twelve Steps of Alcoholic Anonymous has been widely used by other organizations and for other addictive behaviors. Mike O'Neil was given permission to adapt the Steps by substituting the phrase "our human condition" for "alcohol," and to use the adapted version in his book, *Power to Choose: Twelve Steps to Wholeness*.
2. Exodus 20:1-17.
3. For example, Psalm 32:5: "I acknowledged my sin to you [God] and my iniquity I have not hidden; I said, 'I will confess my transgressions to the Lord'; and you forgave the iniquity of my sin."
4. Matthew 6:12, 14.
5. Matthew 22:37-39.
6. See Deuteronomy 6:4-5; 32:1-43; Matthew 25:34-46; John 15:9.
7. Proverbs 13:3.
8. Katherine, *Boundaries*, p. 90.

Chapter 10   Physical Boundaries

1. Katherine, *Boundaries*, p. 15.

Chapter 11   Sexual Boundaries

1. Ruth S. Kempe and C. Henry Kempe, *Child Abuse* (Cambridge, MA: Harvard University Press, 1978), p. 43.
2. Ibid., p. 56.
3. Steven Farmer, *Adult Children of Abusive Parents* (Los Angeles: Lowell House, 1989), p. 10.
4. E. Sue Blume, *Secret Survivors: Uncovering Incest and Its Aftereffects in Women* (New York: Ballantine Books, 1990), pp. 4-5.
5. As reported in *A Guide to What One Person Can Do About Pornography*, published by American Family Association. Dr. Cline's remarks are from an address delivered at the National Consultation on Pornography, Cincinnati, Ohio, 1985.
6. *Sexaholics Anonymous*, (P.O. Box 300, Simi Valley, CA 93062: SA Literature, 1989), p. v. Copyright © 1989 SA Literature.
7. Ibid., p. 8.

Chapter 12   Emotional Boundaries

1. Katherine, *Boundaries*, p. 70.
2. Anne Wilson Schaef, *Co-dependence: Misunderstood—Mistreated* (New York: HarperSanFranciso, 1986), p. 50.
3. Ibid., pp. 50-51.
4. M. Scott Peck, M.D., *The Road Less Traveled* (New York: Simon & Schuster, 1978), p. 17.
5. Katherine, *Boundaries*, pp. 18, 21.
6. From *The Emotional Incest Syndrome: What to Do When a Parent's Love Rules Your Life* by Dr. Patricia Love. Copyright © 1990 by Patricia Love and Jo Robinson.
7. Ibid., p. 9.
8. Ibid., pp. 16, 9.
9. Ibid., pp. 8, 30.
10. Ibid., from subheads, pp. 33-54.
11. Ibid., pp. 25-26.
12. Ibid., pp. 26-27.
13. Katherine, *Boundaries*, p. 27.
14. Love, *The Emotional Incest Syndrome*, from subheads, pp. 98-102.
15. John Bradshaw, *Healing the Shame That Binds You* (Deerfield Beach, FL: Health Communications, 1988), p. 52.

Chapter 13   Models of Unhealthy Boundaries

1. Cloud and Townsend, *Boundaries*, p. 59.
2. Ibid., pp. 59-60.
3. The main points concerning the boundary types that follow—close, distant, rigid, flexible, permeable, and impermeable—have been abstracted from Anne Katherine's book *Boundaries*, pp. 77-82.
4. Ibid., p. 77.
5. Ibid.
6. Ibid., p. 78.
7. Ibid.
8. Ibid. This list of characteristics in this section were derived from Katherine's comments, pp. 79-80.

Chapter 14   Types of People with Boundary Issues

1. Taken from the book, *Boundaries* by Dr. Henry Cloud and Dr. John Townsend, pp. 49-59. Copyright © 1992 by Henry Cloud and John Townsend.

Chapter 15   Resolving the Losses

1. David Damico, *Faces of Rage* (Colorado Springs, CO: NavPress, 1992), pp. 44-56. The following information concerning losses, rage, and performance and control vows are abstracted from this book by permission.
2. Ibid., pp. 59-70.
3. Ibid., p. 24.
4. Ibid., pp. 81-83.
5. Elisabeth Kubler-Ross, *On Death and Dying,* (New York: MacMillan Publishing, 1969).
6. *Alcoholics Anonymous,* p. 449. © The A.A. Grapevine, Inc.
7. Mike S. O'Neil, *Power to Choose: Twelve Steps to Wholeness* (Nashville, TN: Sonlight Publishing, Inc., 1992), pp. 170-172.

Chapter 16   Forgiveness

1. *American Heritage Dictionary of the English Language,* 3d ed., © Houghton Mifflin Company, 1993.